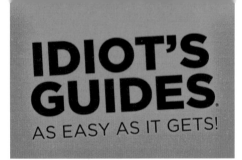

IDIOT'S GUIDES.
AS EASY AS IT GETS!

# Sewing

by Cinnamon Miles

ALPHA

A member of Penguin Group (USA) Inc.

**ALPHA BOOKS**

Published by Penguin Group (USA) Inc.

Penguin Group (USA) Inc., 375 Hudson Street, New York, New York 10014, USA • Penguin Group (Canada), 90 Eglinton Avenue East, Suite 700, Toronto, Ontario M4P 2Y3, Canada (a division of Pearson Penguin Canada Inc.) • Penguin Books Ltd., 80 Strand, London WC2R 0RL, England • Penguin Ireland, 25 St. Stephen's Green, Dublin 2, Ireland (a division of Penguin Books Ltd.) • Penguin Group (Australia), 250 Camberwell Road, Camberwell, Victoria 3124, Australia (a division of Pearson Australia Group Pty. Ltd.) • Penguin Books India Pvt. Ltd., 11 Community Centre, Panchsheel Park, New Delhi—110 017, India • Penguin Group (NZ), 67 Apollo Drive, Rosedale, North Shore, Auckland 1311, New Zealand (a division of Pearson New Zealand Ltd.) • Penguin Books (South Africa) (Pty.) Ltd., 24 Sturdee Avenue, Rosebank, Johannesburg 2196, South Africa • Penguin Books Ltd., Registered Offices: 80 Strand, London WC2R 0RL, England

International Standard Book Number: 978-1-61564-411-7
Library of Congress Catalog Card Number: 2013935155

15  14  13      8  7  6  5  4  3  2  1

Interpretation of the printing code: The rightmost number of the first series of numbers is the year of the book's printing; the rightmost number of the second series of numbers is the number of the book's printing. For example, a printing code of 13-1 shows that the first printing occurred in 2013.

**Note:** This publication contains the opinions and ideas of its author. It is intended to provide helpful and informative material on the subject matter covered. It is sold with the understanding that the author and publisher are not engaged in rendering professional services in the book. If the reader requires personal assistance or advice, a competent professional should be consulted. The author and publisher specifically disclaim any responsibility for any liability, loss, or risk, personal or otherwise, which is incurred as a consequence, directly or indirectly, of the use and application of any of the contents of this book.

Most Alpha books are available at special quantity discounts for bulk purchases for sales promotions, premiums, fund-raising, or educational use. Special books, or book excerpts, can also be created to fit specific needs. For details, write: Special Markets, Alpha Books, 375 Hudson Street, New York, NY 10014.

**Trademarks:** All terms mentioned in this book that are known to be or are suspected of being trademarks or service marks have been appropriately capitalized. Alpha Books and Penguin Group (USA) Inc. cannot attest to the accuracy of this information. Use of a term in this book should not be regarded as affecting the validity of any trademark or service mark.

Publisher: Mike Sanders

Executive Managing Editor: Billy Fields

Acquisitions Editor: Karyn Gerhard

Development Editor: Kayla Dugger

Production Editor: Jana M. Stefanciosa

Book Designers: Sarah Goguen, Kurt Owens

Cover Designer: William Thomas

Indexer: Celia McCoy

Layout: Brian Massey

Proofreader: Laura Caddell

For my girls, Makena and Liberty—may you always strive to become Proverbs 31 women.

*Cinnamon Miles*

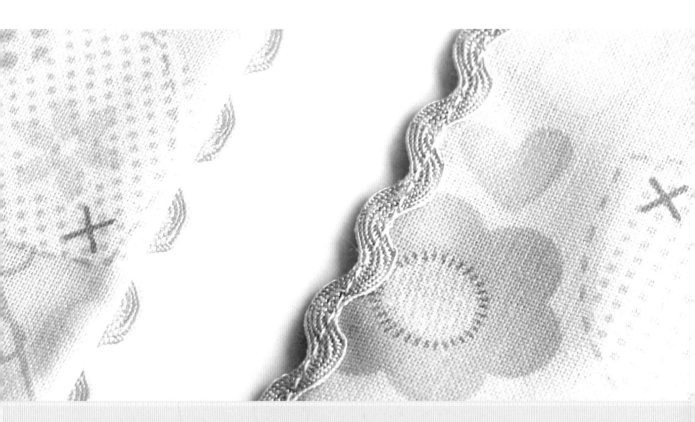

# Contents

# Introduction

*Sewing.* This ability comes a bit more naturally to some people than others, but in either case, it's a skill that should be taught, encouraged, and developed. Sewing is a great creative outlet, and the feeling of accomplishment you get when you make something yourself is indescribable.

Some of my earliest memories are of my mom sewing. We would take trips to fabric stores and pick out lots of great fabrics. Out of those fabrics, she would make me clothes while I sat alongside and created clothes for my Kimberly doll out of the scraps. A friend of my grandma's, who worked for the famous designer Bob Mackie, even gave me scraps of fancy material from his studio that I would use to make dresses for my doll. I still have Kimberly and those original Bob Mackie fabric outfits. They weren't exactly perfect, but they were pretty good for an 8-year-old.

My mom taught me to sew, and it was my passion immediately. I didn't realize it at the time, but I was pretty lucky. She worked for a fashion designer in Santa Monica before I was born, so she was a pretty amazing sewing teacher.

My mom realized I was pretty obsessed with sewing when I accidentally sewed into the tip of my finger while making an outfit and had to go to the doctor to get x-rays to see if the needle was still inside. The next day, I told her I had to keep working on my project and needed her help replacing the needle. She just smiled.

Many years later, when I started Liberty Jane Clothing, I was on my own, sewing and selling. The lessons and advice I learned as a young girl came back quickly. Fortunately, I was then able to start to build a team of amazing seamstresses. As I asked them about their early experiences, I discovered that our journeys were very similar—their moms played a big part in their early sewing lessons.

As I put this book together, I tried to create it in a way that anyone could follow. Whether you're trying to learn on your own for yourself or to teach your children, this book is written for you.

The chapters are designed to give you a step-by-step guide with simple-to-follow instructions. I begin with the very basics by walking you through the anatomy of the machine and how it functions. I then provide lessons that build on each other, so that by the time you reach the end of this book, you'll know everything from how to sew a simple stitch to how to insert a zipper. I've made sure to include lots of close-up images to really help you understand the practical sewing tips taught in this book.

I also supply a variety of projects in this book to help you practice your sewing. The projects at the end of each chapter use the skills taught in the sections of that chapter, while the projects in the last part are a way to practice a number of different skills you learned throughout the book. Don't feel intimidated, especially when you get to the intermediate-level projects—just take them one step at a time, and you'll be amazed at what you're able to create!

My hope is that the journey of learning to sew is not stressful at all, but encouraging and fun! I wish you all the best in your sewing journey.

Cinnamon

## Acknowledgments

I am so grateful for this amazing opportunity to pass along the things I've learned. Thank you to Marilyn Allen, my agent, whose advice and guidance have gotten me to this point. Your encouragement and support have been amazing. I'd like to say a special thanks to Karin Pascho and Melinda Schlimmer, who worked with me to create the amazing projects included in this book. Your skill and talent have been such an inspiration, and your friendships are invaluable. I'd also like to thank my mom, Victoria Arnold, not just for being an amazing mother, but for taking the time out of her busy day to teach me to sew. You have passed along a great gift. A shout-out to my three kids, Jordan, Makena, and Liberty—thank you for putting up with the crazy schedule and long hours; you guys are the best. And of course I want to thank my amazing husband, Jason Miles—your support and encouragement have meant the world to me. I'm so excited to be on this lifelong journey with you.

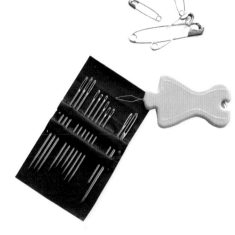

# Part 1
# Getting Started

# Chapter 1

## Before You Begin

Tools of the Trade
Understanding Fabric

# Pins and Needles

So many pins, needles, cushions, and threaders are available to choose from at the fabric store, it's hard to know where to start. The following are a few basic types you need to get started. You can add to your collection as you discover what types you do and don't like and which things you use the most.

1. **Steel straight pins with colorful glass heads** are easy to see and use, and they won't melt under a hot iron.

2. A **magnetic "pincushion"** is one of my most favorite tools. Just swipe it over your sewing table or even the floor and watch it magically pick up any loose pins!

3. A **stuffed pincushion** allows pins to stand upright so they're easy to grab when you only have one free hand. It also keeps the point of the pins clean and sharp because they're not exposed to dust and moisture. Some varieties even attach right to your sewing machine.

4. **Safety pins** are used to pull elastic through casings. They can also be used in place of pins if you're working on a large project you want to fold up and save for later.

5. **Hand-sewing needles** come in a variety of sizes for both the eye and the length/width of the needle. It's good to have a variety pack of needles on hand; you never know when you might need a super-small one for something delicate or a larger one for thick, tough fabric.

6. A **needle threader** can be a useful tool if you have trouble seeing that tiny needle eye or have shaky hands. You can use it on either a hand-sewing needle or a machine needle.

# Measuring Tools

Measuring and marking tools are something you'll want to have on hand when working on sewing projects. You can choose from a variety of tools, based on your personal preference. Here are a few of the essentials:

1. A **seam gauge** is a small ruler with a sliding marker. It's used to measure out even hems or evenly spaced pleats or tucks.

2. **Washable cloth-marking pencils** are used to mark on fabric and can be removed with water. These are used for transferring guidelines on patterns to the cut pieces.

3. A **clear, plastic ruler** is used for basic measuring, marking buttonholes, lining up the grain, and marking pleats. It is also used with a rotary cutter to make long, straight cuts.

4. A **water-erasable marker** is used in the same way as a marking pencil. It is also used to mark while fitting a garment on a person. Be cautious not to iron over these marks—the heat will set them in the fabric, making them permanent!

5. A **flexible tape measure** is used for taking measurements of the body so you can create properly sized garments. It's usually 60 inches (152.4 cm) in length and has centimeter markings on the opposite side.

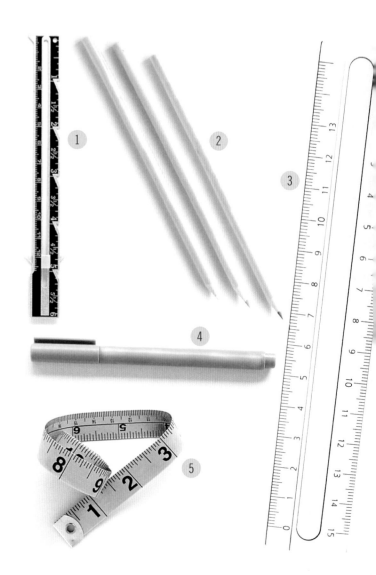

# Cutting Tools

Good-quality cutting tools are key to successful sewing, so buy the best shears and scissors you can afford and keep them sharp. That way, you'll avoid the frustration of dull blades and wasted fabric!

1. **Tiny 4-inch (10 cm) embroidery snips or scissors** have a very fine, super-sharp point that's perfect for trimming thread close to the fabric.

2. **Fabric shears** are what you'll use to cut large pieces of fabric. A pair of high-quality shears that can be sharpened can last a lifetime. However, be sure you only cut fabric with them; using them to cut paper or other materials can dull the blades!

3. **Paper scissors** or old shears can be used to cut paper, patterns, tape, and fusible products. They can't be used on fabric because the blades aren't sharp enough to result in a smooth, clean cut.

4. **Pinking shears** are used to trim seams to keep edges from raveling. It's good to have them on hand, but if you don't, you can finish your edges with some of the techniques taught in this book.

5. A **seam ripper** is used to remove stitching. The name is a bit misleading, because there isn't any ripping happening at all—it merely involves sliding the hook under the stitches and letting the small blade at the base cut through the thread. No matter how accomplished you might be at sewing, you'll have to take out a seam at some point, so this tool is a must.

6. A **rotary cutter** with a **self-healing cutting mat** is used to cut through many layers of fabric. You can get it in several sizes (the rotary cutter pictured is on the small side). It has a very sharp blade, so always use it with extreme caution.

# Pressing Tools

Oftentimes, pressing is the step that gets skipped over in a sewing project. Take the time to press when your instructions recommend it—it's key for creating a nicely finished product. For the best results, press on the wrong side of the fabric and use a pressing cloth when necessary to protect both the iron's surface and your fabric.

1. A narrow **sleeve board** is a small version of an ironing board that's used to press small areas or seams in narrow spaces.

2. A full-size **ironing board** is a safe surface on which you can iron your fabric. Be sure to keep the cover of this essential tool clean so you don't transfer sticky residues or marks onto your fabric.

3. The curved end of a small **wooden point turner** is used for finger pressing. You use your fingertip to firmly press and slide the curved end along the fabric fold to create a crisp crease or line.

4. A **rolled towel** is used to press curved seams or sleeve seams open without creasing the fabric. It's similar to a tailor's ham or seam roll, but most beginning sewers don't have those tools on hand and can cheaply and easily use a rolled towel in place of them.

5. A **pressing cloth** is a thin piece of cotton fabric used between an iron and the main fabric to protect both the iron's surface from sticky residues due to fusible webs and the fabric from iron shine.

6. A **steam iron** is the most essential tool for pressing! Choose a high-quality iron that has a wide range of temperatures and can press with or without the steam function. Unless otherwise stated in the sewing instructions, you'll use a steam iron for pressing.

# Fabric Defined

Choosing the right fabric can make or break your project. It is essential to understand what makes up a piece of fabric and what it is meant to be used for. There is a large variety of fabrics out there to choose from, so understanding these elements will help you to make the right choices for your project.

- The threads that run parallel to the selvage (lengthwise) are the **warp threads.** The threads that run crosswise to the selvage, and are woven through the warp threads, are the **weft threads.**

- The **selvage** is the finished edge of the fabric. It is tightly woven and won't fray, but generally it has a bit of a different color or is left unprinted.

- The **right side** is the outside or finished side of the fabric—it's the side you want to be visible. You can tell which side is the right side pretty easily on a printed fabric.

- The **wrong side** is the inside or unprinted side of the fabric. This is the side that is unseen on a finished project.

- The **bias** is the line of the fabric which lies 45 degrees from the selvage and falls between the lengthwise and crosswise grains. A woven fabric has a bit of stretch when cut in the direction of the bias.

| Yardage | Inches/cm |
|---|---|
| 1/8 | 4 1/2 / 11.4 |
| 1/4 | 9 / 23 |
| 1/3 | 12 / 30.5 |
| 3/8 | 13 1/2 / 34.25 |
| 1/2 | 18 / 45.75 |
| 5/8 | 22 1/2 / 57 |
| 2/3 | 24 / 61 |
| 3/4 | 27 / 68.5 |
| 7/8 | 31 1/2 / 80 |

1 yard = 36 inches (91.5 cm)

## Yardage Conversion Chart

Fabric is available to purchase in a variety of widths. It is rolled onto bolts; you take the bolts to a cutting counter to have the specific amount needed measured and cut off the bolt.

Sewing patterns have charts that specify the amount of fabric needed. Most yardage measurements will be for a standard 44- to 45-inch-wide fabric. But what should you do if you want to use a fabric that is, for example, 60 inches wide? The chart below will help you to make easy conversions if you plan to use a fabric that comes in a different width.

| Fabric Width | 35-36" | 39" | 41" | 44-45" | 50" | 52-54" | 60" |
|---|---|---|---|---|---|---|---|
| Yardage | 1 3/4 | 1 1/2 | 1 1/2 | 1 3/8 | 1 1/4 | 1 1/8 | 1 |
| | 2 | 1 3/4 | 1 3/4 | 1 5/8 | 1 1/2 | 1 3/8 | 1 1/4 |
| | 2 1/4 | 2 | 2 | 1 3/4 | 1 5/8 | 1 1/2 | 1 3/8 |
| | 2 1/2 | 2 1/4 | 2 1/4 | 2 1/8 | 1 3/4 | 1 3/4 | 1 5/8 |
| | 2 7/8 | 2 1/2 | 2 1/2 | 2 1/4 | 2 | 1 7/8 | 1 3/4 |
| | 3 1/8 | 2 3/4 | 2 3/4 | 2 1/2 | 2 1/4 | 2 | 1 7/8 |
| | 3 3/8 | 3 | 2 7/8 | 2 3/4 | 2 3/8 | 2 1/4 | 2 |
| | 3 3/4 | 3 1/4 | 3 1/8 | 2 7/8 | 2 5/8 | 2 3/8 | 2 1/4 |
| | 4 1/4 | 3 1/2 | 3 3/8 | 3 1/8 | 2 3/4 | 2 5/8 | 2 3/8 |
| | 4 3/4 | 4 | 3 7/8 | 3 5/8 | 3 1/4 | 2 7/8 | 2 3/4 |
| | 5 | 4 1/4 | 4 1/8 | 3 7/8 | 3 3/8 | 3 1/8 | 2 7/8 |

**Note:** You might need to adjust the amounts for fabrics that have stripes, plaids, or large prints so the pieces line up. Also, if you're extending one measurement and narrowing another, check to be sure that the width of your pattern pieces will still fit on the piece of fabric.

# Fabric Types

You choose fabric for a sewing project based on its look, feel, and use. Because wading through the many fabric types available can be pretty overwhelming, here's a list of the basic types and their general use.

First, a word about what makes fabrics different. Woven fabric includes everything from lightweight to thick and heavy, but the defining factor is that it's woven on a loom. Knitted fabrics are either warp knitted or weft knitted. Warp knit is done by machine and is commonly found in tricot, milanese, and raschel varieties. Weft knit can be done either by hand or by machine and is commonly found in double-knit, interlock, jersey-knit, purl-knit, and rib-knit varieties. Of the two, warp knitted has the most stretch.

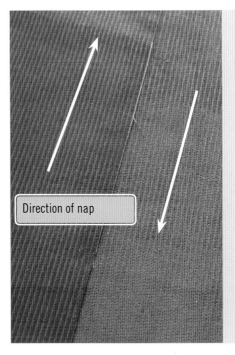

Direction of nap

This piece of corduroy fabric is cut and laid out with the nap facing in opposite directions. See the slight difference in the shade of the color?

Corduroy, velvet, suede, and flannel are some of the types of fabrics that have *pile* or *nap*. The threads on the surface of the fabric are raised and can be smoothed down with your hand. When you slide your hand in one direction, causing the threads to lay flat, it feels smooth; when you slide it in the other direction, causing the thread to stand up, it feels rough.

Your pattern pieces must be cut following the nap as well as the grain. When pieces are sewn together with the nap going in different directions, the color of the fabric will look different. To make sure this is done, you may need additional fabric for a pattern because pieces need to be laid out in a specific direction—be sure to look for that measurement.

- **Solid cotton** is one of the most basic types of fabric and comes in a variety of weights and solid colors. This popular fabric doesn't have stretch and can be machine washed and dried (though doing so will shrink it).

- **Printed cotton** is probably the most popular fabric choice because it's cute and easy to sew with, comes in a variety of weights, and doesn't have stretch. Printed designs can range from tiny to large, so pay special attention to matching the larger designs on the seams when using printed cotton.

- **Wool** is a woven fabric made from sheep fleece that's spun into yarn. Wool is used to make coats, tailored garments, and home décor projects, among other things. Any garments or projects using this fabric usually have to be dry cleaned.

- **Fleece** is a soft, fuzzy, knit fabric with a bit of stretch. You can find thick and thin types of fleece, as well as sweatshirt fleece, in which the fabric is smooth on one side.

- **Corduroy** is a woven fabric with raised parallel lines, called *wales,* that can be narrow or wide. This fabric is easy to sew with, is machine washable, and has great durability.

- **Knit** fabric is soft, stretchy, and very comfortable. You can find knits in a variety of weights with two-way or four-way stretch. This fabric can be used to make all sorts of clothing items and is machine washable.

- **Silk** is a lightweight, delicate fabric often used in clothing items. This fabric can be sheer or slippery, and is usually meant to be dry cleaned only. The cut edges on silk will fray, so the seams need to be finished well.

# Preparing Your Fabric

You've chosen your pattern and decided on fabric. Now, all you need to do is prepare the fabric, and you can begin sewing!

## Preshrinking

When making clothing, preshrinking the fabrics is essential. You can do this in several ways.

Before purchasing fabric, be sure to note the fabric-washing instructions on the end of the bolt. Some fabrics are preshrunk by the manufacturer.

Wash the fabric, and even the notions, the same way you would after you'd wear it. You definitely want to have the shrinking happen before you make the project instead of after.

If the fabric is dry clean only, have it cleaned prior to cutting it out, since dry-cleaned items can sometimes shrink. You can also steam press a dry-clean-only fabric. Simply lay out your fabric, steam evenly over your fabric horizontally or vertically, and let it dry flat. The steam released will shrink up the fabric.

**Note:** Before preshrinking, be sure to note which side of the fabric is the right side. Some fabrics look very similar on both sides, so once the sizing is washed away, it can be hard to determine which side is which. To avoid this problem, make a small mark with a permanent marker on the corner of the fabric.

## Checking the Fabric Grain

To check if the fabric is on grain, do the following:

1. Pull on the crosswise or warp threads near the end of the piece of fabric.

2. As you pull them, you will see the fabric bunch up like a gather along the cut end. Trim along this line to have a straight edge.

3. Fold the fabric lengthwise, and line up the selvage edges and crosswise ends. If the fabric is smooth, it is on grain; if lays unevenly, it is off grain.

To fix fabric that's off grain, you can steam press the fabric while it's still folded by securing the selvage edges and pressing toward the fold.

Even if the fabric is on grain, you should go over it with an iron to remove large wrinkles from prewashing. You want the fabric to lay flat when pinning and cutting the pattern pieces.

## What Is a Fat Quarter?

A fat quarter is an 18 x 20- or 18 x 22-inch (45.75 x 51 cm) piece of woven cotton fabric often used for patchwork or appliqué.

The standard width of quilting cotton fabric is 44 inches (111.75 cm). To make a fat quarter, the fabric is cut at $^1/_2$ yard (45.75 cm), which results in a piece that measures 18 x 44 inches (45.75 x 111.75 cm). The piece is then cut in half again to create two pieces that are more square than rectangular. A $^1/_4$ yard (23 cm) cut off the bolt would measure 9 x 44 inches (23 x 111.75 cm). This gives the user a much more versatile piece to work with.

Fat quarters come individually packaged or in cute bundles of coordinating prints and solids. You can find them in the same section as the quilting cotton at your local fabric store.

# Chapter 2

## Know Your Machine

# Anatomy of a Sewing Machine

While several different types of sewing machines exist, most have the same basic parts and features. Here's a general breakdown of the features of a sewing machine (refer to your machine's manual for specifics).

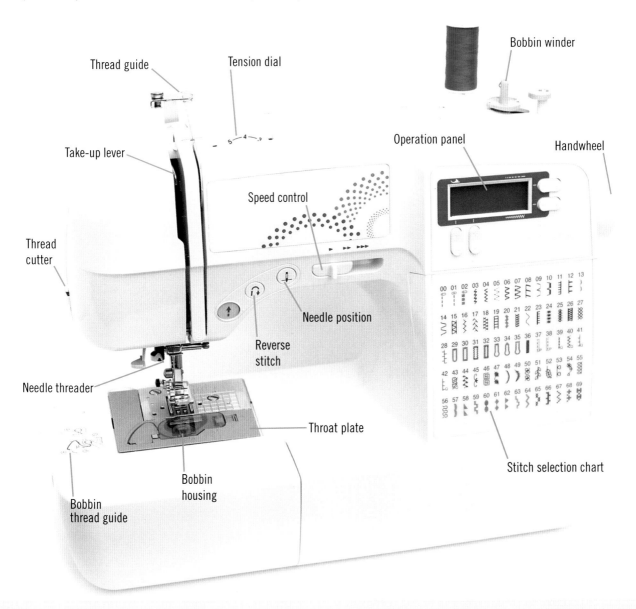

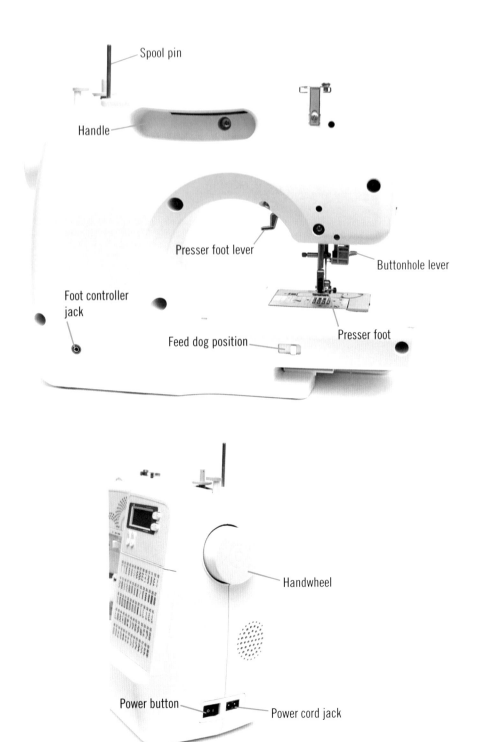

Spool pin

Handle

Presser foot lever

Buttonhole lever

Foot controller
jack

Feed dog position

Presser foot

Handwheel

Power button

Power cord jack

# Threading a Sewing Machine

While the first time you thread your machine may seem a bit overwhelming, once you do it a few times, it'll become second nature. Each machine may thread a bit differently, but the basic thread path is the same. To get you started, here's a general description.

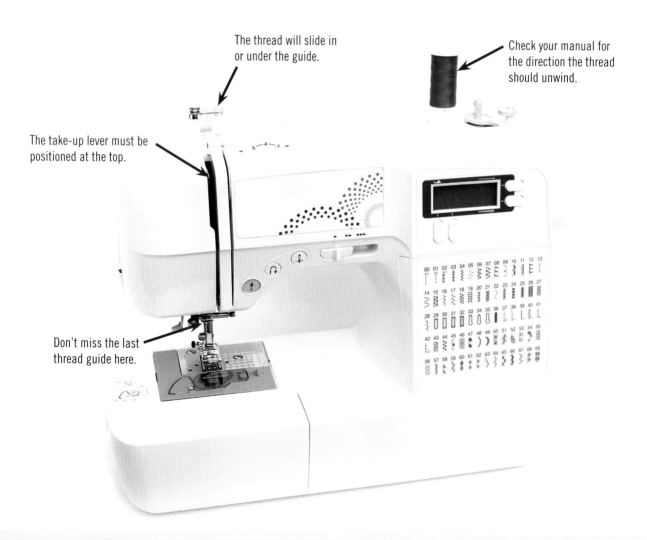

The thread will slide in or under the guide.

Check your manual for the direction the thread should unwind.

The take-up lever must be positioned at the top.

Don't miss the last thread guide here.

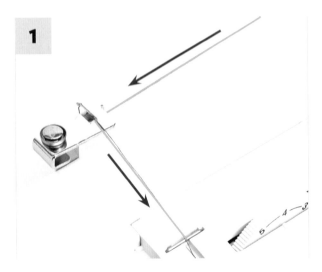

**1**

Place the thread on the spool. Pull the thread off of the spool and guide it through the first thread guide mounted on top of the machine.

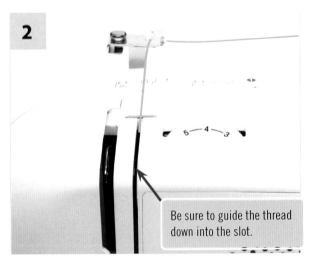

**2**

> Be sure to guide the thread down into the slot.

Move the thread along the thread guide. Pull the thread forward and slide it into the narrow slot, guiding it toward the bottom of the machine.

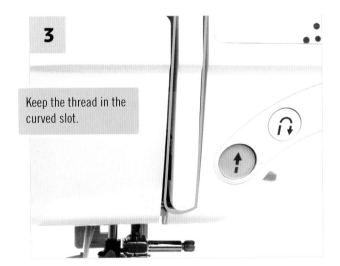

**3**

> Keep the thread in the curved slot.

In the narrow slot, pull the thread around the curve and back up to the top of the machine. This will bring you to the take-up lever.

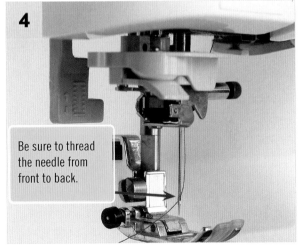

**4**

> Be sure to thread the needle from front to back.

Slide the thread through the take-up lever and back down to the needle. (The thread will go back into the same narrow slot.) Pull it through the final thread guide, just above the needle, and thread the needle from front to back.

## Variations You Might See on a Machine

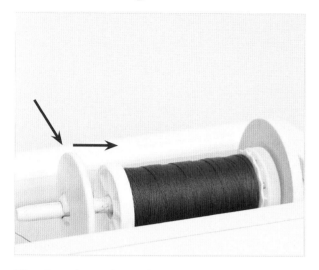

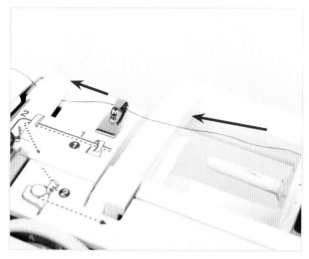

The thread spool can also lay flat on the machine. This type will have a spool disc to keep thread spool secure.

This is a different type of thread guide with two slots to guide the thread through; they are not raised like the example in step 2. The thread goes through in the same manner.

### Thread Tips

- Invest in high-quality thread; it will last longer, resist breaking, and produce strong seams.
- Polyester thread is a good choice for all-purpose sewing. You can also use threads based on the type of fabric you're working with—for example, cotton with cotton and silk with silk—but it's not necessary.
- Rayon thread is generally used for machine embroidery.
- Thread that's wound in a crisscross manner is less likely to get tangled on the spool pin and unwinds more evenly.

# Machine Needles

Different types of fabrics require different types of needles. Although a universal needle can work on a variety of fabric types and weights, it's best to use the proper needle for your project to achieve the best results. Here are some of the common types, along with instructions on how to replace your needle.

Universal needles can be used on a variety of fabrics, both knit and woven.

Microtex or sharp needles work with silk, foils, and faux leathers.

Twin needles are used to create two parallel rows of stitching (for example, jeans topstitching).

Jersey or ballpoint needles are used on knits and stretch fabrics.

Lower the presser foot, or remove the foot to have more space. To release the needle, loosen the needle clamp screw by hand or with the small screw driver that came with your machine.

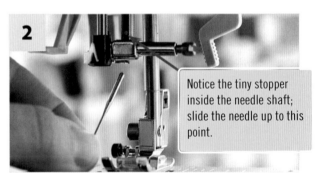

Notice the tiny stopper inside the needle shaft; slide the needle up to this point.

Pull out the needle. Notice the direction the flat side of the needle fits in the slot, toward the back or the front. Insert the new needle into place, and tighten the screw to secure.

# Loading a Bobbin

Now that you've got your upper thread all figured out, you'll need to learn how to wind and load the bobbin. Here, I show you the basics for understanding your bobbin. Be sure to look at your machine manual for specifics—some might even have an illustrated diagram that shows you exactly what path to follow.

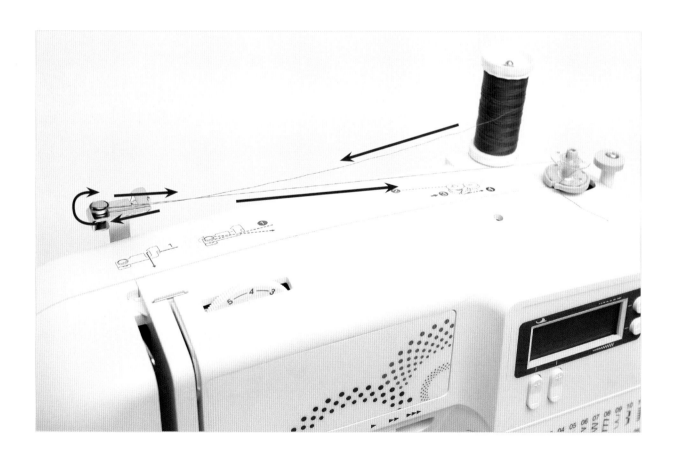

Lots of bobbin storage options are available to keep your bobbins neat and tidy!

The images in this example show both metal and plastic bobbins. Bobbins are specific to your machine model, so make sure you know which one your machine uses when looking to purchase additional bobbins.

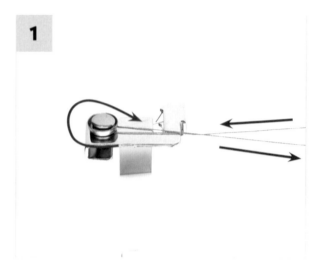

**1**

Bring the thread around the front of the bobbin winder thread guide. Wrap it around the bobbin in the direction shown for your machine (clockwise here).

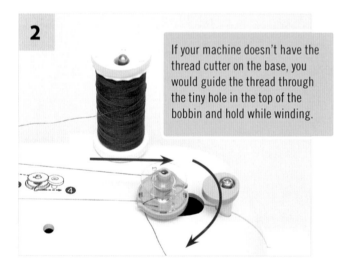

**2**

If your machine doesn't have the thread cutter on the base, you would guide the thread through the tiny hole in the top of the bobbin and hold while winding.

Guide the thread to the bobbin and wrap it around the bobbin two or three times in a clockwise direction. Pull the thread through the slit in the base.

**3**

Push the bobbin winder to the right. It will click into place. For some machines you may have to push the lever toward the stationary bobbin winder instead.

Next, follow the steps based on your type of bobbin.

## Top-Loading Bobbin

**1** Remove the bobbin housing cover. Place the bobbin into the hole, following the guide for the direction the thread should unwind.

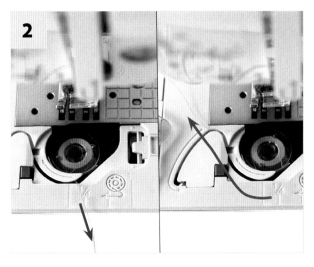

**2** Slide the thread into the slit. Be sure to start at the front of the opening so the thread goes through the tension-adjusting spring. Follow the path up and around.

**3** Pull thread to the end of the path along the tiny thread cutter. Hold the bobbin with your finger and pull to cut the thread.

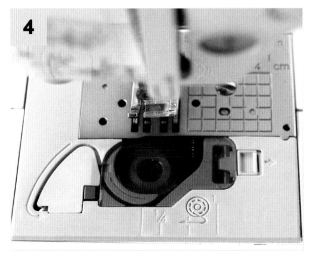

**4** Replace the bobbin cover, being careful to insert it in the proper direction. The machine will draw up the bobbin thread on the first stitch.

## Front-Loading Bobbin

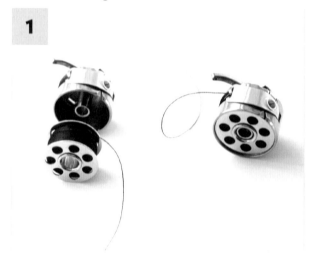

Slide the bobbin into the bobbin case, with the thread unwinding in the direction stated in your manual. Pull the thread back into the slit and under the thread guide at the top of the case.

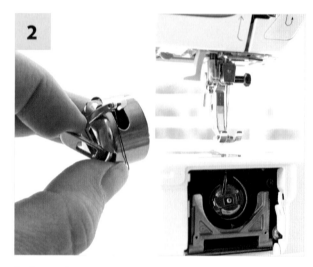

Pull out the small lever on the case to hold the bobbin in place. Slide the combined bobbin and bobbin case into the bobbin housing, paying close attention to the fit. It should click into place.

### A Closer Look at the Needle Plate

The needle plate, also called a *throat plate,* is marked with lines to help you sew a straight seam. You refer to these markings for seam allowances.

The marking for ⅝ inch (1.5 cm) up at the top is the standard for most sewing projects, with the exception of doll clothes, which are usually set at ¼ inch (.6 cm). A corresponding line marking is at the front of the plate to keep your fabric lined up correctly.

The four small rows of metal teeth under the foot are called *feed dogs.* These gently pull the fabric under the foot as you sew.

# Sewing Machine Feet

A variety of feet are available for most sewing machines. For most beginner-level projects, you'll use the standard foot (also called a *zigzag foot*) that comes on your machine. As you progress and are ready to try other types of projects, though, you'll likely want to use the appropriate type of sewing machine foot. The following discusses the different types and gives a short tutorial for replacing one on your machine.

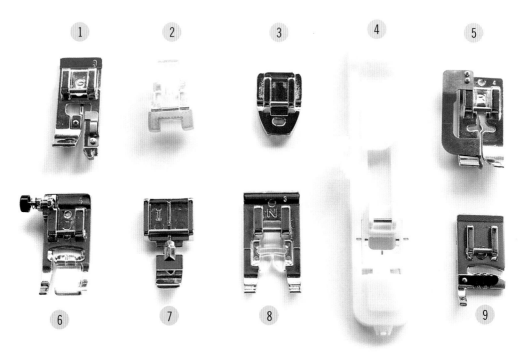

1. **Overcasting foot:** This foot is designed to sew just past the edge of the fabric in a zigzag motion and finishes the edge. The extended part guides the edge of the fabric, while the tiny metal guide inside holds the fabric flat. It works great with knits!

2. **Button fitting foot:** This foot allows you to sew on a two- or four-hole button. It works by using a zigzag stitch set at zero length.

3. **Invisible zipper foot:** Also called a *concealed zipper foot*, this foot is used specifically for invisible zippers. Invisible zippers are easy to install and are hidden under the edge of the fabric, making them invisible from the outside.

4. **Buttonhole foot:** This long, rectangular foot is designed to automatically sew buttonholes at a variety of lengths. The button fits into the back to determine the size.

5. **Blind stitch foot:** This foot is designed with a guide to allow you to stitch a blind hem by keeping the needle at the correct distance from the hem. A blind hem is barely visible from the right side of the fabric.

6. **Zigzag foot:** This is the standard, all-purpose foot that comes on the machine. It has a wide opening for the needle, which can accommodate a variety of stitch styles.

7. **Zipper foot:** This foot is used to insert all types of zippers; it's designed to allow the needle to sew right along raised zipper teeth. You can also use it to insert piping.

8. **Monogramming foot:** This foot is used to create monograms by using the free-motion sewing technique. It has a clear area that allows you to see the stitching under the foot as you sew.

9. **Cording foot:** This foot has small groves in it to guide the trim and keep it exactly where you want it. It works with both a straight or zigzag stitch.

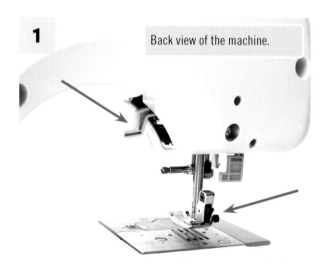

Raise the presser foot. Push the button or lever on the back to release the foot.

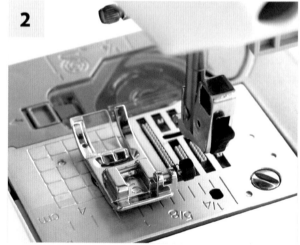

Slide the foot out. Position the new foot just under the presser foot holder, and lower to attach.

# Adjusting the Tension and Stitches

Several methods are available for adjusting the tension and stitches on a sewing machine (refer to your manual for specifics). Here are the buttons and dials to look for when using a digital control panel:

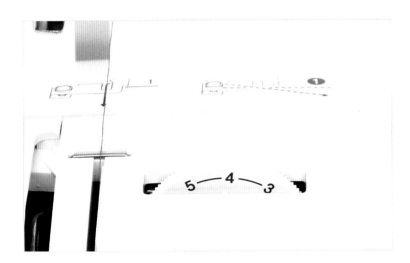

To adjust the tension, turn the tension dial. Higher numbers make it looser; lower numbers make it tighter.

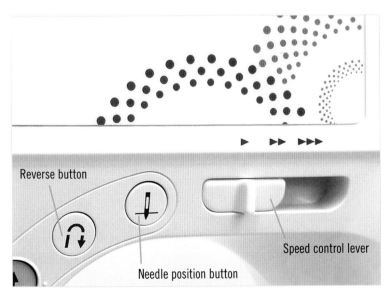

Reverse button

Needle position button

Speed control lever

A reverse button is standard on machines, but not all have the needle up/down position or speed control buttons. These are two very helpful features for sewing perfect stitches.

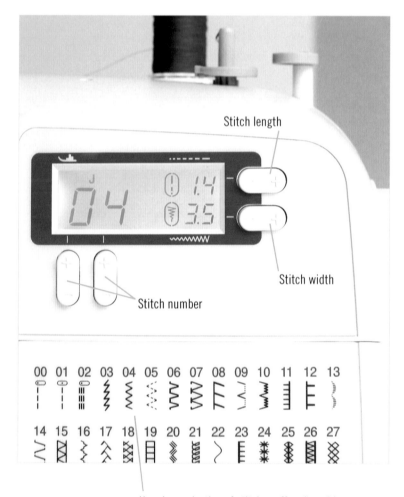

Stitch length

Stitch width

Stitch number

00 01 02 03 04 05 06 07 08 09 10 11 12 13

14 15 16 17 18 19 20 21 22 23 24 25 26 27

Here is a selection of stitches offered on this machine; the stitch number is identified above each stitch.

Each type of stitch has a corresponding number, noted on the front panel of the machine. Underneath the digital control panel are two buttons to select the stitch number you want. The left button is for the first number; the right button is for the second number. Push up or down to get the desired number.

The set of buttons to the right of the digital display control the stitch length and width. In this case, the top button is for the length (note the dotted lines in the red area above) and the bottom controls the width (note the zigzag line in the red area below).

# Part 2
# Start Sewing

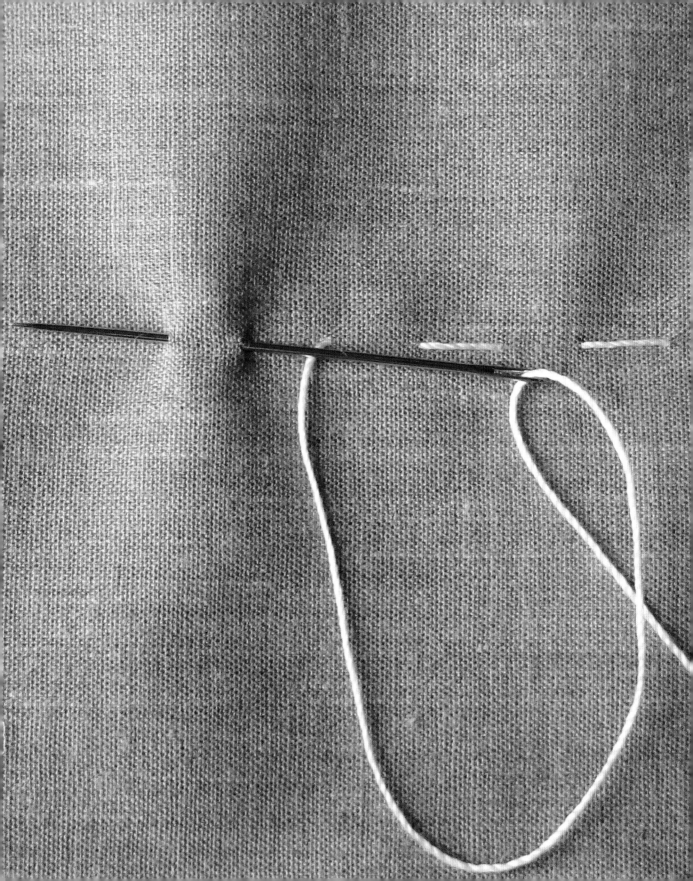

# Chapter 3

## Stitching Basics

Straight Stitch
Backstitch
Zigzag Stitch
Tension
Basic Hand Sewing
Practice Project: Bookmark

# Straight Stitch

Sewing a straight line is the basis for most sewing projects and is easy to master with a bit of practice. Taking the time to learn this skill is important because uneven seams affect the overall fit or look of your project.

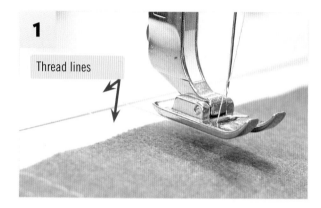

**1**

Thread lines

Be sure the upper thread is under the foot but on top of the fabric, the bobbin thread is under the fabric, and both threads are pulled to the back behind the foot.

**2**

Lower the presser foot, and push the foot pedal to begin sewing. Use your hands to guide the fabric from the front side of the machine. Do not pull from behind the foot; this can bend the needle or cause uneven stitches.

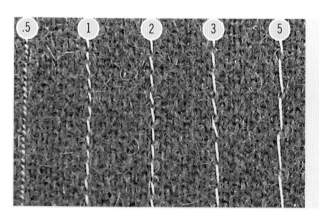

Now let's practice some straight stitches! Set your stitch length at .5 and sew a straight line. Stop sewing, lift the presser foot, and cut the threads. Slide the fabric over ¹/₄ inch (.6 cm). Change the stitch length to 1, and sew another row of straight stitches. Continue this process while adjusting the stitch length for each row.

# Backstitch

Sewing a backstitch will secure (or knot) your seam. To sew this stitch, you will be using the backstitch button or lever (depending on your model).

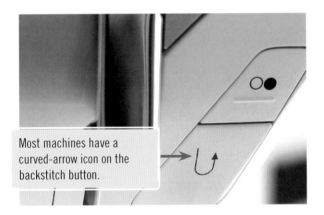

Most machines have a curved-arrow icon on the backstitch button.

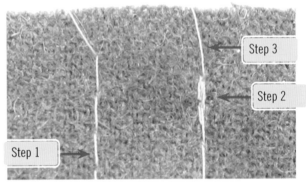

Step 3

Step 2

Step 1

To sew the backstitch:

1. Begin by stitching two forward stitches.

2. Stop sewing, then push the backstitch button and hold it down while sewing two backward stitches.

3. Release the button and continue sewing forward.

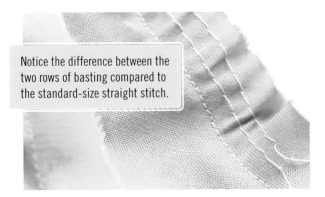

Notice the difference between the two rows of basting compared to the standard-size straight stitch.

### Basting: What's That All About?

The basting stitch is used to hold pieces of fabric together temporarily. It is also used to create ease or gathers. To sew this stitch, select the highest number on the stitch length selector, usually 5.

Remember, basting is meant to be removed—don't backstitch!

# Zigzag Stitch

A zigzag stitch has both functional and decorative uses. There are multiple variations depending on the stitch width and length you select. To sew this stitch, select the stitch on the stitch selector, then use the stitch length and stitch width selector to set the size of the zigzag.

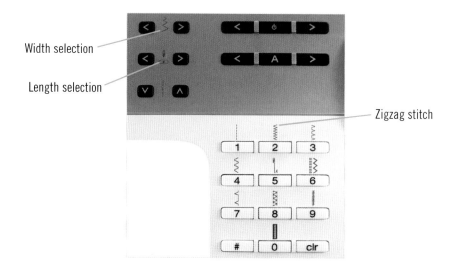

Width selection

Length selection

Zigzag stitch

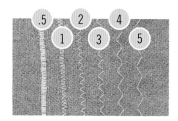

The shortest stitch length setting creates what is called a *satin stitch*. Changing the stitch length causes the stitches to be either closer together or more spread out. All the stitches shown here are sewn at the same width; only the length has been adjusted.

Changing the stitch width adjusts the width of the zigzag. The stitches above are all sewn at the same length; only the width has been adjusted.

# Tension

At some point, your machine will have issues with tension. In the world of sewing, *tension* refers to the pressure that's put on the thread coming from the top. The thread tension dial on the front of a sewing machine is used to adjust the tension. Different fabrics and stitches require different amounts of tension. If your stitching looks uneven or inconsistent, you may have an issue with your tension setting.

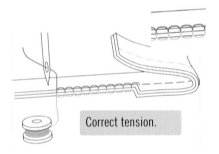

Correct tension.

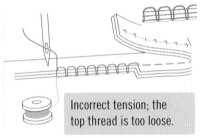

Incorrect tension; the top thread is too loose.

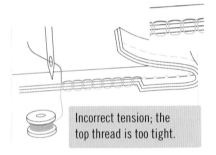

Incorrect tension; the top thread is too tight.

This shows balanced thread pulling from both the top thread and the bobbin thread; it's the ideal tension.

In this image, the top thread is too loose. It is pulled all the way through by the bobbin. You would see the thread on the underside of the fabric.

Here, the top thread is too tight. The bobbin thread is pulled up to the top. You would see the bobbin thread on the topside of the fabric.

My best advice as it relates to tension issues is to take out both the bobbin and the top thread and rethread the whole thing, being sure to guide the thread through the guides and take-up lever. Check to see if your bobbin is wound tight and smooth; sometimes they can get tangled on the spool. You can also check the bobbin area for lint buildup and remove it if necessary. Finally, you can replace the needle—even a new needle could be faulty.

# Threading a Needle

**1**

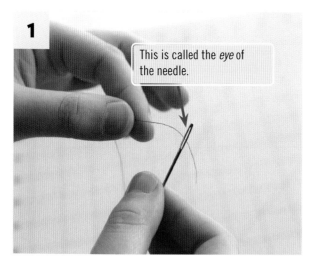

This is called the *eye* of the needle.

With sharp scissors, cut the end of a piece of thread. Poke the thread through the eye at the top of the needle.

**2**

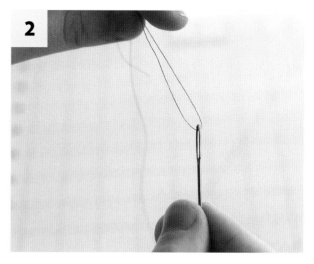

Pull the thread through the eye, and bring up to join the other end of the piece of thread.

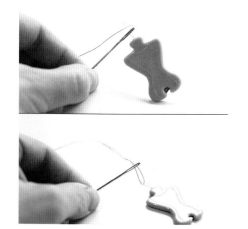

**Threading a Needle with a Needle Threader**

Insert the wire loop through the eye of the needle.

Slide the thread through the wire loop.

Pull the wire loop back through the needle.

Continue to pull the thread all the way through.

Now you're ready to sew by hand!

# Securing the Thread

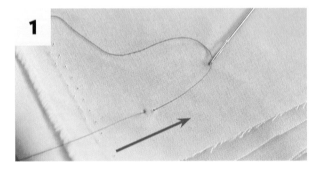

**1**

Poke the needle into the fabric and pull back through to the top. Be sure to hold the loose thread with a tight thumb grip.

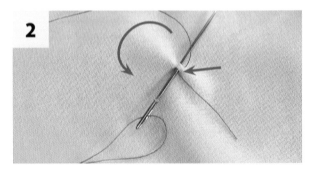

**2**

Repeat the same stitch, being sure to guide the needle under the short tail.

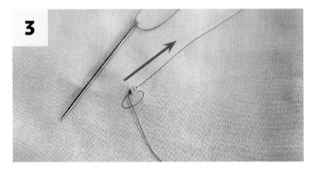

**3**

Pull the thread all the way through, watching as a small loop is formed around the tail. Pull tight.

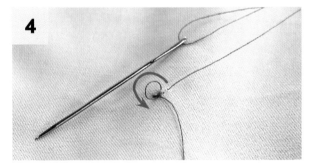

**4**

Repeat the stitch a third time, looping around the tail once more. Pull tight, and trim the tail as close to the knot as possible.

## Hand-Sewing with Thimbles

Thimbles are designed to protect your finger as you push a needle through a fabric. When you perform this process with a thimble-covered finger tip, you'll see how easily the needle slides through even the thickest of fabrics.

Thimbles that cover the entire tip of the finger can be made of metal or rubber and are typically used by dressmakers. Thimbles with an opening can be made from metal, rubber, or even leather and are typically used by tailors.

# Types of Stitches

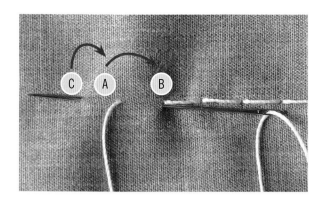

**Backstitch:** This stitch is used to create a strong seam. Start by bringing the needle up from the back of the fabric at point A. Insert your needle back down at point B. Bring the needle up a stitch length in front at point C. Insert the needle back down at point A. Continue along until you've reached the end of the seam.

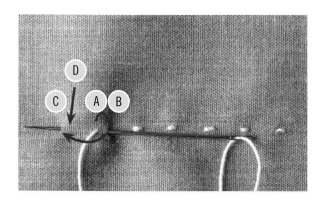

**Prick stitch:** Also called a *pick stitch,* this is a variation of the backstitch used to sew in a zipper by hand or reinforce a seam. Start by bringing the needle up from the back of the fabric at point A. Insert your needle back down at point B. Bring the needle up a stitch length in front at point C. Insert the needle back down at point D, and continue along until you reach the end of the seam. The top stitches will look like small pricks, and the bottom stitches will be a longer stitch.

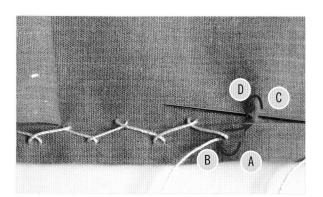

**Catch stitch:** This stitch is used to sew a hem with hardly any stitch showing on the outside. Working from left to right and with your needle always pointing left, make a small stitch through the hem fold (A to B). Place the next stitch $1/_4$ inch (.6 cm) away on the backside of the garment, taking up just a few threads (B to C to D). Continue the next stitch on the hem fold, repeating the crisscross pattern.

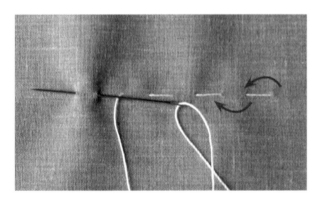

**Running stitch:** This stitch is used to create a strong seam. Bring up your needle from the backside and weave your needle in and out of the fabric, spacing your stitches about ⅛ inch (.3 cm) apart. The stitch should look the same on both sides of the fabric.

**Whipstitch:** This stitch is used to hold two folded edges together. Sew the stitches from front to back near the fold, taking your needle around to the back layers. Keep your stitches close together. This is also a great stitch for felt edges!

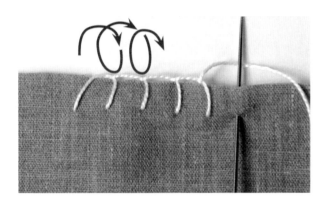

**Blanket stitch:** This stitch is used to sew an edge stitch on a blanket or piece of felt. Start by bringing your needle up to the front, about ¼ inch (.6 cm) away from the edge. Working left to right and staying on the front side of the garment, place your needle about ¼ inch (.6 cm) away from the first stitch and from the edge. Push the needle through the garment, but come up again by going through the thread loop. Pull gently to create the blanket stitch.

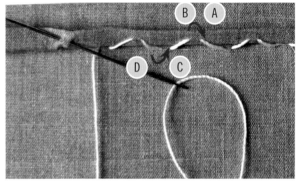

**Blind hem stitch:** Similar to a catch stitch, this stitch is used to sew a hem with hardly any stitch showing on the outside of the garment. Start by folding back the pressed-up hem so only ⅛ inch (.3 cm) shows past the fold. Working right to left, take up a small stitch in hem allowance (A to B). Make next stitch ¼ inch (.6 cm) away on the back of the garment, taking up only a few threads (C to D). Continue the next stitch on the hem allowance and then again on the backside of the garment.

# Practice Project: Bookmark

A personalized bookmark is a perfect first sewing project. Using fabrics that don't fray or stretch, such as felt or wool felt, make this project simple, stress free, and fun!

Simply choose two coordinating colors for the main bookmark and accent with either a cut fabric strip or ribbons of any width. You can make them in your favorite colors or the colors of a popular sports team. The possibilities are endless!

## What You Need

- Knowledge of straight stitching and zigzag stitching
- Level of difficulty: Easy/beginner
- Two 8×10 (20.25×25.5 cm) sheets *or* two $1/8$-yard (11.5 cm) pieces or small scraps felt or wool felt fabric in different colors
- 8 $1/2$-inch piece $1/2$-inch- to $3/4$-inch-wide (1.25 to 2 cm) ribbon (or decorative fabric of your choice)
- Sewing machine
- Thread
- Fabric scissors
- Straight pins
- Ruler or measuring tape

**1**

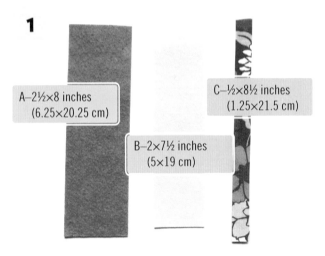

A–2½×8 inches
(6.25×20.25 cm)

B–2×7½ inches
(5×19 cm)

C–½×8½ inches
(1.25×21.5 cm)

Measure and cut the two rectangles, A and B, out of felt or wool felt. Cut one piece of ribbon or fabric for the top layer, C.

**2**

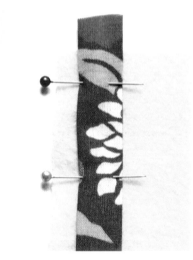

Place layer C on top of layer B ¼ inch (.6 cm) from the left edge, and pin in place. Zigzag stitch over the edge of layer C down the length of the strip, and backstitch at each end to secure.

**3**

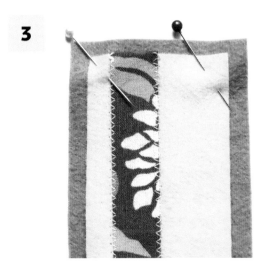

Fold the edge of layer C under at the top and bottom so it is under layer B. Place layer B on top of layer A; center them so the exposed edges are even. Pin to secure.

**4**

Be sure to keep C tucked under B when straight stitching!

Straight stitch on all four sides of layer B. Backstitch at the beginning and end of each row of stitches. Your stitching lines will crisscross at the corners.

# Chapter 4

## Seams and Hems

Sewing and Pressing a Straight Seam
Seam Finishes
Sewing a Hem
Practice Project: Infinity Scarf

# Sewing and Pressing a Straight Seam

Sewing a basic seam is the first sewing technique you should learn. Once you can do this simple task, you will be able to work on a variety of projects.

Pressing a seam may seem like an unnecessary step, but don't skip it! The end result will look much better when you've taken the time to do it right.

## What You Need

- Standard foot attachment
- Two pieces of fabric
- Straight pins
- Iron

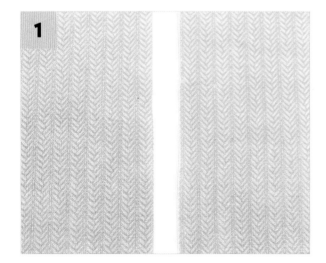

**1**

Lay out your fabric with the right sides facing up.

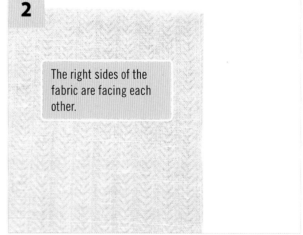

**2**

The right sides of the fabric are facing each other.

Place one piece of the fabric on top of the other piece, lining up the cut edges on the right. The wrong side of the fabric is now visible.

**3**

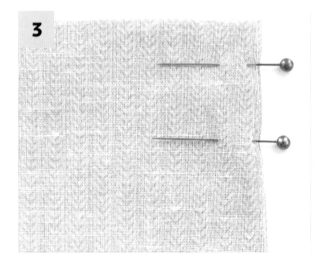

Slide pins into the fabric along the seam edge, down through both layers, and back up through the top. Pin every few inches to hold the fabric in place.

**4**

Remove the pin just before it reaches the foot. Sewing on a pin can break your needle!

⅝-inch (1.5 cm) seam marking

Line up the edge of the fabric with the ⅝-inch (1.5 cm) seam marking on the throat plate. With the stitch selection set to straight, begin sewing a straight line.

**5**

This area is called the *seam allowance.*

When you've sewn a straight line along the entire length of the piece, you've created the seam. Be sure to backstitch at the beginning and at the end to secure your stitching.

**6**

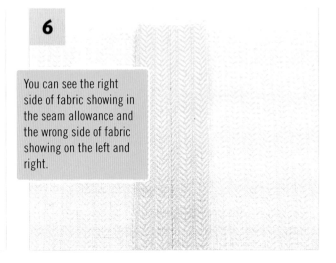

You can see the right side of fabric showing in the seam allowance and the wrong side of fabric showing on the left and right.

Open up the fabric and lay it flat with the right side facedown. Use an iron to open the seam and press it flat.

# Seam Finishes

Properly finished seams are key to making your project look its best. You may think, *No one will see that part, so who cares?* But finished seams not only make your project look good, they also help with durability and prevent fraying.

Here are two basic methods for nicely edged seams. My preference of the two is the zigzag—it's quick and easy, and every machine can do it.

## What You Need

- Zigzag foot attachment
- Scissors
- Pinking shears
- Iron

### Pinking Shears

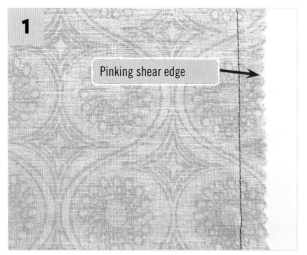

Sew a straight seam at a ⅝-inch (1.5 cm) seam allowance. Trim the seam allowance to ¼ inch (.6 cm) with pinking shears.

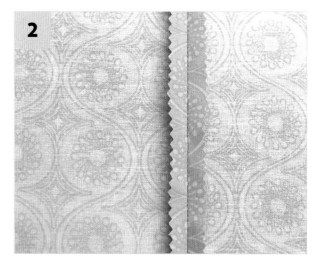

Open the seam with the wrong side of the fabric facing up. Press the seam open.

## Zigzag Stitch

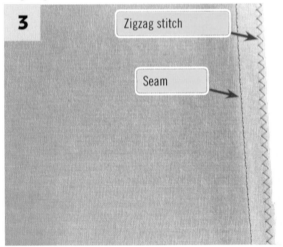

**3** Zigzag stitch

Seam

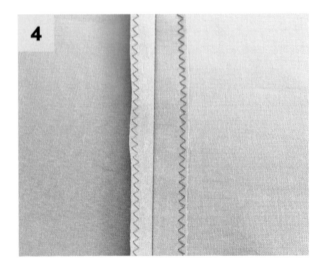

**4**

Before sewing your seam, sew a standard zigzag around the edges of your cut fabric. Sew your seam as directed in your pattern or project instructions.

Open up the seam and press it flat. Trim any stray threads close to the zigzag stitching from the fabric.

### Say Hello to Your New Best Friend: The Seam Ripper!

A seam ripper is an invaluable tool to have on hand! Its tiny, sharp point allows you to take out even the tiniest seams. To begin, carefully slide the tip under the thread and, with a little pressure, split the thread. Skip a few stitches and pull out another. Then just grip the thread, and it should slide right out!

# Sewing a Hem

Finishing well is important in all areas of life, including sewing! A crisp, clean hem can add a professional touch to any item and eliminate frayed edges.

A double-turned hem is probably the easiest type to learn and do well. This hem is made from two simple folds and hides the raw edge. You can make this type of hem at any width. (The following example is shown at $1/2$ inch [1.25 cm].)

## What You Need

- Standard foot attachment
- Seam gauge
- Straight pins
- Iron

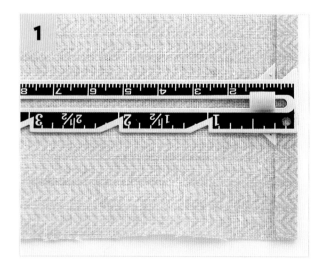

**1**

Fold and press the edge of your fabric under $1/4$ inch (.6 cm) using an iron. Use the seam gauge to create an even fold.

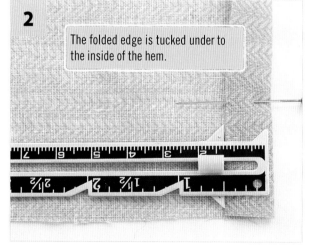

**2**

The folded edge is tucked under to the inside of the hem.

Fold under again at the desired hem width. (This example shows a $1/2$-inch [1.25 cm] hem.) Secure the hem with pins.

**3**

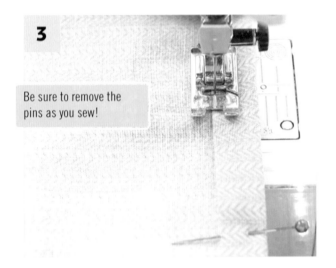

Be sure to remove the pins as you sew!

Sew a straight stitch right along the upper folded edge.

**4**

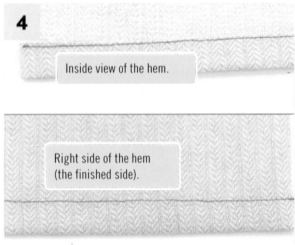

Inside view of the hem.

Right side of the hem (the finished side).

Sew along the entire length of the hem. Backstitch at both the beginning and the end.

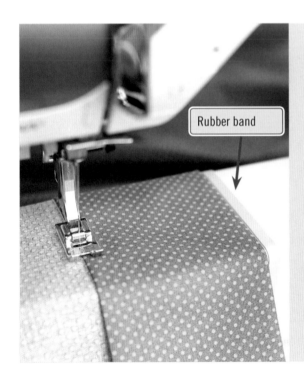

Rubber band

### Tips for Sewing a Perfectly Straight Larger Hem

Some projects may require a larger hem—for example, a curtain may have a 3-inch (7.5 cm) hem—but the standard markings on the throat plate usually only go up to 1 inch (2.5 cm). Here are a few tips for creating a larger straight hem:

- Measure out from your needle to the desired length of the hem.
- Use a rubber band or a piece of easy-to-remove painter's tape to mark the line on your machine.
- Line up the edge of your hem with this new guide as you sew. Be sure to remove the rubber band or tape immediately so you don't leave any residue on your machine!

# Practice Project: Infinity Scarf

An infinity scarf is a long tube of fabric sewn into an enclosed circle. It is worn by simply wrapping twice around the neck and has a gentle, slouchy look. Be sure to choose a lightweight fabric, like cotton voile or silk, or a thin knit so the scarf will look its best!

## What You Need

- Knowledge of straight seams
- Level of difficulty: Beginner/easy
- $^2/_3$ yard (61 cm) 60-inch-wide (152.5 cm) fabric or 1 $^2/_3$ yards 45-inch-wide (114.25 cm) fabric
- Straight pins
- Iron
- Sewing machine

**1**

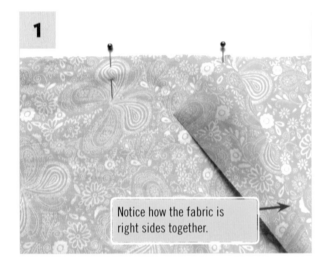

Notice how the fabric is right sides together.

**2**

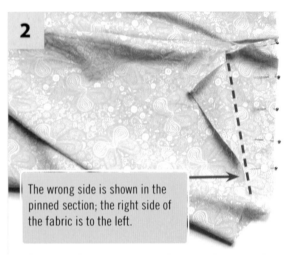

The wrong side is shown in the pinned section; the right side of the fabric is to the left.

Cut one rectangle 60×25 inches (152.5×63.5 cm). Fold in half lengthwise, and pin. Sew a straight seam along the edge, leaving 3 inches (7.5 cm) open at each end.

Turn the tube right side out. Match up the open ends with the right sides together, and pin the entire circle. Be sure the 3-inch (7.5 cm) opening is lined up. Straight stitch the two ends of the tube together.

**3**

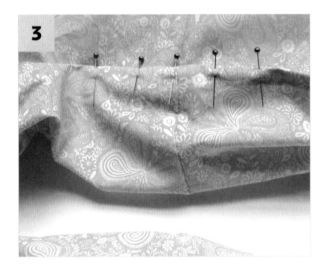

Pull through and press the opening flat. Pin the opening together with the raw edges tucked inside. Sew a topstitched straight seam to close the opening, making sure to sew right along the edge.

# Chapter 5

## Corners and Curves

Curved Seams
Sewing Corners
Practice Project: Peter Pan Collar Embellishment

# Curved Seams

Curved seams may seem challenging, but you can create great-looking curves by following some simple steps.

When sewing inward curves, you have to clip the seam allowance so the fabric can stretch. You have to notch the seam allowance of outward curves to reduce bulky lumps. Both techniques are easy to learn. Just be sure you have a nice pair of small, sharp scissors!

## What You Need

- Standard foot attachment
- Sharp scissors
- Straight pins
- Pinking shears (optional)
- Iron

## Inward Curve

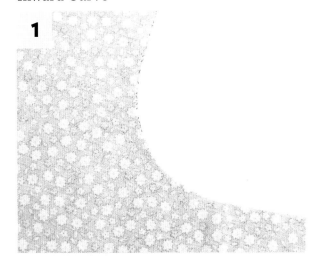

**1**

This is an inward curve cut into two pieces of fabric. The fabric is sewn with the right sides together.

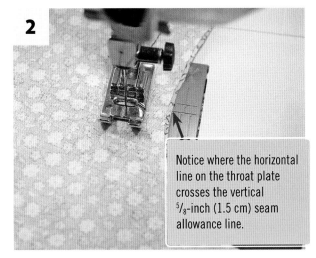

**2**

Notice where the horizontal line on the throat plate crosses the vertical ⅝-inch (1.5 cm) seam allowance line.

With a straight stitch and a ⅝-inch (1.5 cm) seam allowance, carefully sew the seam, guiding the fabric to follow the curve.

**3**

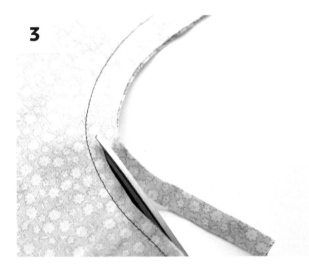

Trim the seam to ¼ inch (.6 cm), cutting through both layers of the fabric.

**4**

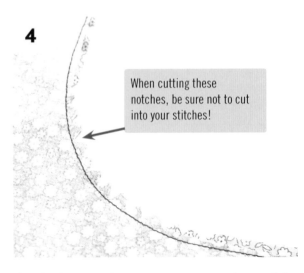

When cutting these notches, be sure not to cut into your stitches!

Grade the seam by trimming just one layer of the seam allowance close to the stitching line, and notch the curve. If your curve is gentler, you can just cut straight snips.

**5**

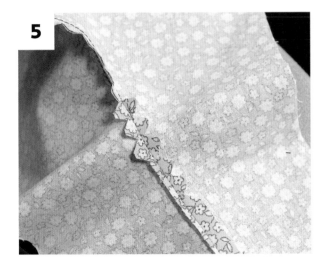

Press the seam open as far into the curve as you can. Be careful not to crease the fabric.

**6**

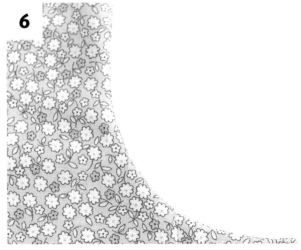

Turn the fabric right side out and press the seam flat.

## Outward Curve

**1**

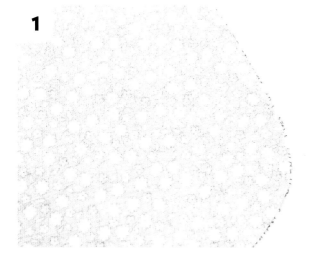

This outward curve is a gently rounded corner. The fabric is cut and sewn with the right sides together.

**2**

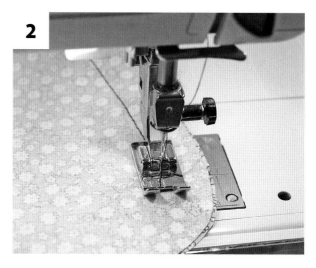

Sew a straight stitch and gently guide the fabric to turn as you round the curve. Be sure to keep the seam allowance lined up at all points throughout the curve.

**3**

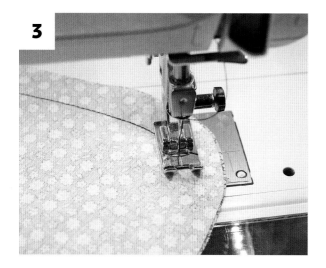

When sewing a tight curve, you may have to pause, raise the foot, and pivot the fabric slightly. Then lower the foot and continue sewing.

**4**

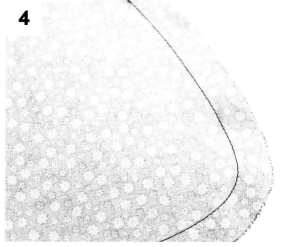

Notice the smooth, even seam along the curve. Be careful to keep it from looking like a corner with a point.

**5**

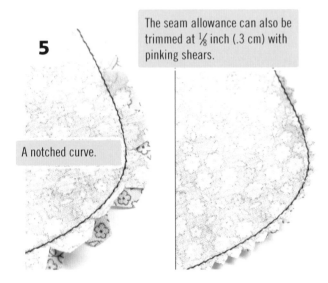

The seam allowance can also be trimmed at ⅛ inch (.3 cm) with pinking shears.

A notched curve.

Trim the seam allowance and notch the curve. Notice the uneven notching for the top and bottom layers; this keeps the seam strong.

**6**

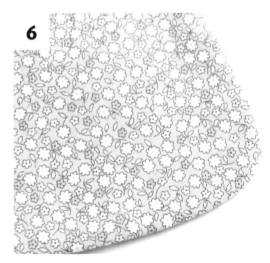

Press the seam open as much as possible. Turn the fabric right side out, and press the seam flat.

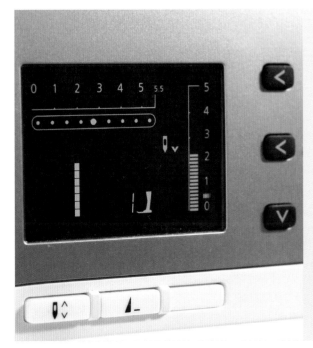

### Needle Up or Needle Down?

Most sewing machines have a selection button to keep the needle in the down position when you stop sewing.

Notice the button with the small icon that has the needle and both the up and down arrow? The digital display shows you which of the two choices you have selected. Sewing with the needle down is key to smooth seams on curves and corners.

If your machine is not digital, you can turn the handwheel on the side of the machine to keep the needle down while turning your fabric.

# Sewing Corners

Sewing a clean, crisp corner can be a bit tricky, but with the right technique, it is easy to master!

Pivoting is the key to a great point on an outside corner as well as a nice-looking inside corner. You will see these types of corners used most on square necklines, pillows, or purses.

## What You Need

- Standard foot attachment
- Sharp scissors
- Marking tool (like a pencil)
- Straight pins
- Point turner or pencil
- Iron

### Outside Corner

This shows an outside corner cut at a 90-degree angle. The fabric is sewn with the right sides together.

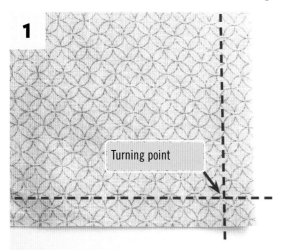

**1**

Turning point

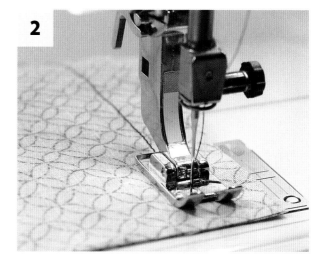

**2**

Mark the seam allowance ($\frac{5}{8}$-inch [1.5 cm]) on the fabric. Measure from both sides to create the intersecting turning point.

Sew a straight seam until you reach the corner mark. Stop sewing with the needle in the down position.

**3**

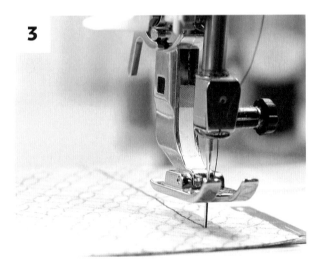

Raise the presser foot. Keep the needle down and poking through the fabric.

**4**

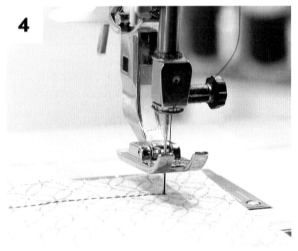

With the needle down, turn the fabric so the other side edge lines up with the seam guideline. Lower the foot and continue sewing.

**5**

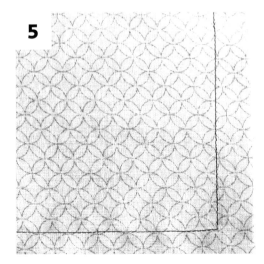

This is how your straight-stitched seam with a pivoted corner should look—very crisp. By pivoting, you create a continuous seam without the bulk of backstitching.

**6**

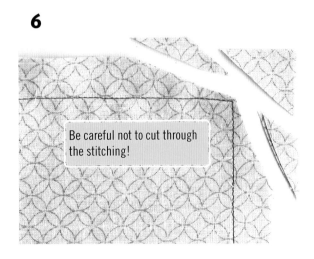

Be careful not to cut through the stitching!

Now you need to trim the corner. First cut off the point, then angle in toward the corner to reduce bulk.

**7**

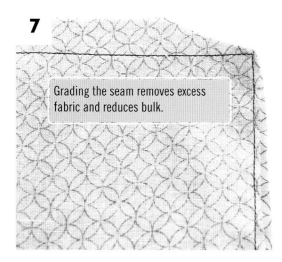

Grading the seam removes excess fabric and reduces bulk.

Grade the seam on both edges (this is sometimes referred to as "layering" the seam). Trim the top layer of fabric to $\frac{1}{8}$ inch (.3 cm) and the bottom to $\frac{1}{4}$ inch (.6 cm).

**8**

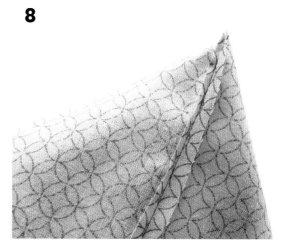

Press the seam open as close to the point as you can. Use your fingers to press open the point.

**9**

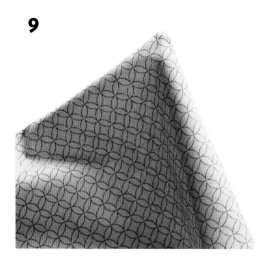

Turn the fabric right side out. Use a point turner or a pencil to carefully push out the corner to a point.

**10**

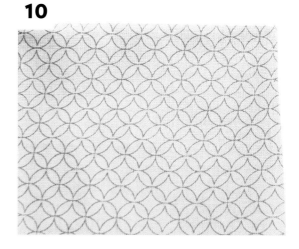

Press the corner flat. Notice the finished corner has a clean, sharp point.

## Inside Corner

This is how you create an inward corner cut into two pieces of fabric. The fabric is sewn with the right sides together.

**1**

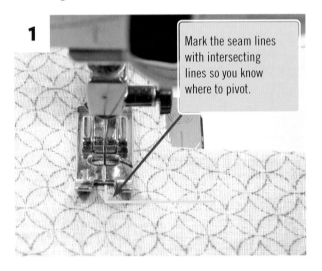

Mark the seam lines with intersecting lines so you know where to pivot.

To sew an inside corner, straight stitch up to the point where the lines intersect; this is where you will pivot the corner.

**2**

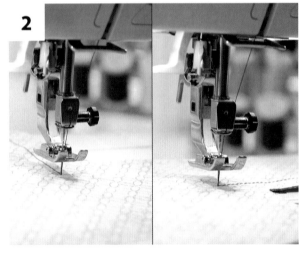

To pivot, first be sure the needle is down in the fabric. Raise the foot and turn the fabric. Line up the seam allowance, lower the foot, and continue sewing.

**3**

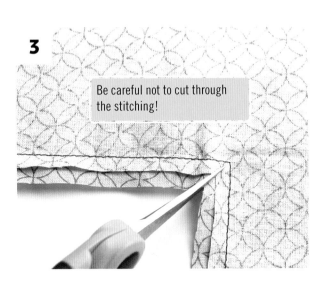

Be careful not to cut through the stitching!

Trim and grade the seams. Using small, very sharp scissors, clip into the corner as close to the stitching as possible.

**4**

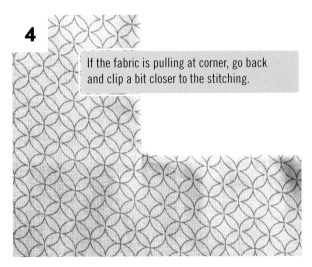

If the fabric is pulling at corner, go back and clip a bit closer to the stitching.

Press the seams open and turn right side out. Press again to create a crisp corner.

# Practice Project:
# Peter Pan Collar Embellishment

Add a vintage feel to a plain tank top or tee with the addition of a Peter Pan collar!

## What You Need

- Knowledge of sewing curved seams, corners, and finishing seams
- Level of difficulty: Beginner/easy
- Basic, store-bought, classic tank top
- $1/4$-yard (23 cm) piece fabric (such as cotton, lace, or chiffon) for collar
- Sewing machine
- Thread
- Scissors
- Straight pins
- Iron
- Measuring tape, pencil, and paper

**1**

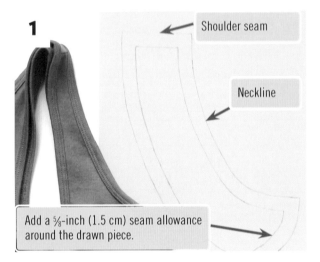

Shoulder seam

Neckline

Add a ⅝-inch (1.5 cm) seam allowance around the drawn piece.

Fold top in half at the center front, and line up shoulder seams. Trace the neckline and shoulder seam on a piece of paper. Following the neckline curve, draw another line 2 inches (5 cm) out, and curve it up at the center front.

**2**

Trim the corner seam.

Notch the curve.

With the fabric layered right sides together, cut four pieces. Sew a straight stitch at ⅝-inch (1.5 cm) seam allowance, starting at the center front and following the outside curve up to the shoulder. Pivot in toward the center.

**3**

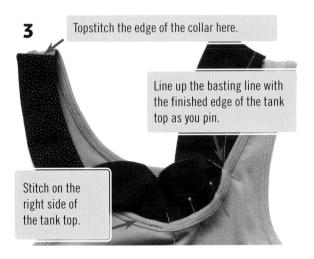

Topstitch the edge of the collar here.

Line up the basting line with the finished edge of the tank top as you pin.

Stitch on the right side of the tank top.

Turn the collar right side out, and press it flat. Baste the open edge, and clip the seam allowance. Place the underside of the collar on the bottom side of the tank top neckline, matching the shoulder seam and center front. Straight stitch.

**4**

For a more finished look, zigzag the raw edge of the collar down to the tank on the inside. Fold the collar over, and press it flat.

# Chapter 6

## Trims and Finishes

# Types of Trim

Trims come in a variety of shapes and sizes. They can be sewn in the seam or applied to the outside edge. Trims like bias tape can be used to cover raw edges, while trims like ribbons and lace are used to add detailed embellishment. Overall, trims are a great way to express your personal style and give your project a finished and professional look.

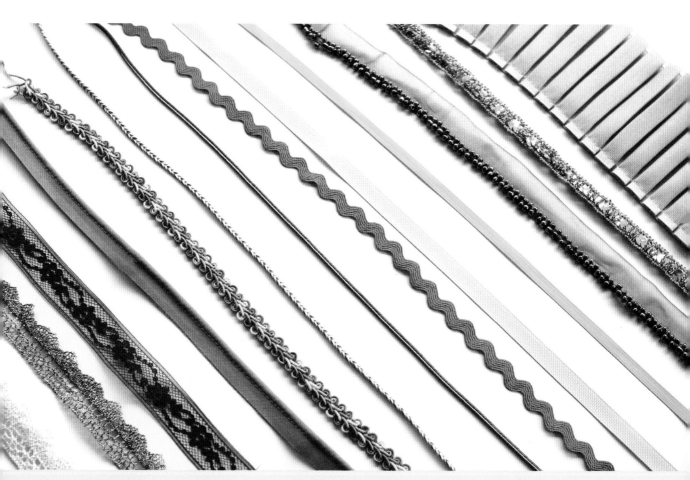

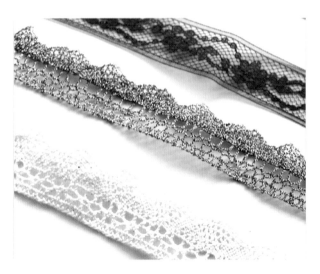

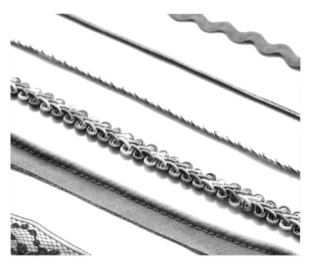

Crocheted lace and metallic lace can be sewn in the seam or on the outside edge. Hem tape, shown here in lace, is generally used on the inside edge of a hem.

Piping is sewn in the seam and is a great way to add a finished look to a pillow. Braided trims and cording are applied on the outside and are used as accents on a project.

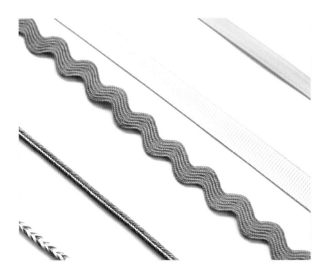

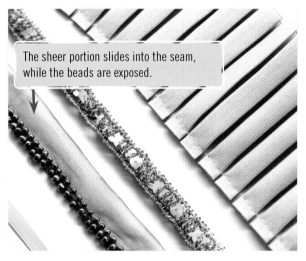

The sheer portion slides into the seam, while the beads are exposed.

Rickrack trim can be sewn in the seam or on the outside, with a straight stitch down the center. Grosgrain and satin ribbon are sewn along the edges on the outside of the fabric.

Beaded trim is sewn in the seam, while sequined trim is sewn on the outside. The pleated grosgrain ribbon trim is sewn in the seam along the stitched edge.

# Sewn In Seam

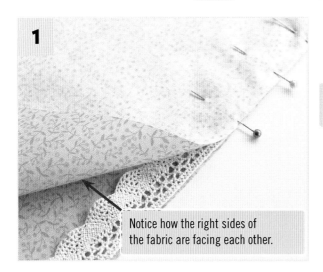

**1**

Notice how the right sides of the fabric are facing each other.

Place the trim in between the two layers of fabric. The finished edge of the trim will point away from the raw edge. Pin.

**2**

The seam allowance will be determined by the size of the trim.

Straight stitch through all three layers, removing the pins as you sew. Be sure to keep the trim flat and to guide it gently with your fingers.

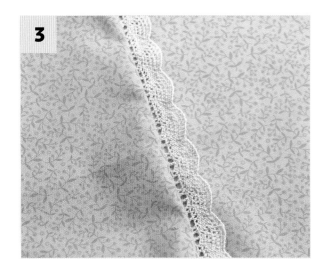

**3**

Open the fabric to see the trim extending out of the seam. You can sew the seam at different widths to have less trim show. Trim the seam on the inside.

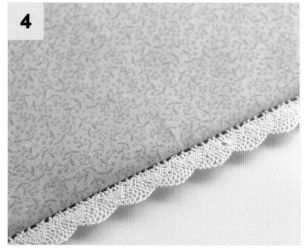

**4**

Press the seam with the wrong sides of the fabric together. Depending on the project, you can top-stitch or edge stitch for extra durability.

# Edge Trims

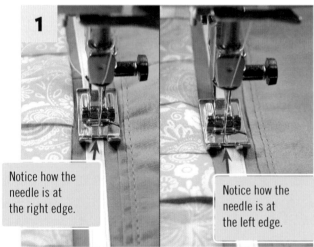

**1** Notice how the needle is at the right edge.

Notice how the needle is at the left edge.

Mark your line on the fabric and either pin or use a fusible product to hold the ribbon in place while you sew.

**2**

Straight stitch along both edges of the ribbon. Take your time in order to sew a straight and even line; a wobbly line of stitches will distract from the trim.

A variety of trims can be sewn on the edge of a seam or the surface of a fabric. These are generally sewn on with a simple straight stitching line. They can be purely decorative or used to cover the spot where two fabrics meet. In this example, I use a narrow ribbon for the trim.

### Two Ways You Can Use Rickrack Trim

Some trims can be sewn in the seam or on the surface; it's really up to your personal preference!

Rickrack trim is a great example of a trim being used two ways. On the left side of the image, you can see the trim is sewn in the seam and just the half circles poke out—a cute detail! On the right of the image, you can see the trim is sewn right at the edge, but sewn on top.

When sewing rickrack, sew a straight seam right down the center. For your project, you'll want to use thread the same color as the rickrack.

# Piping

Piping is a trim or embellishment you can use to define the edges of a project. Many sizes and colors are available premade, but it's also easy to make your own. You can follow the steps to make bias strips and then simply fold them in half over the desired size of cording and baste to secure. One of the most common uses of piping is to edge a pillow. It adds a finished look and a pop of color!

## What You Need

- Zipper foot attachment
- Seam ripper
- Piping
- Straight pins
- Small scissors

**1**

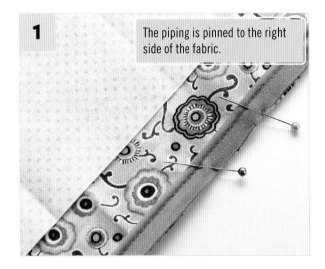

The piping is pinned to the right side of the fabric.

Place the raw edge of the piping trim along the raw edge of the right side of the fabric. Pin in place along the seam allowance.

**2**

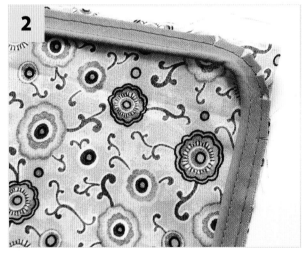

Baste stitch to hold the piping in place. Cut small slits into the seam allowance to gently curve around a corner. The curve should be smooth, not folded.

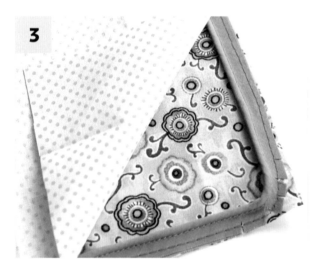

**3**

Layer the other piece of fabric on top with the right sides together. Match up the raw edges.

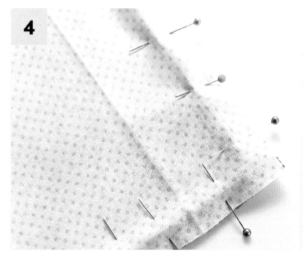

**4**

Pin through all three layers. It's easiest to pin through the seam allowance, not through the cording.

**5**

With the zipper foot attached, guide the foot just along the lump from the cord. Straight stitch as close to the piping cord as you can.

**6**

Turn the fabric right side out and gently push out the corners. If any basting stitches are showing on the piping, simply remove with a seam ripper.

# Using Bias Tape

Bias tape is used in lots of home-decorating projects. It gets its name because of how it's made—the fabric is cut on the bias, or diagonally across the grain. This gives the trim a bit of stretch, which is helpful for curving around corners smoothly. Bias tape can be used on its own or to make piping, giving raw edges a nice, finished look.

## Binding Edges

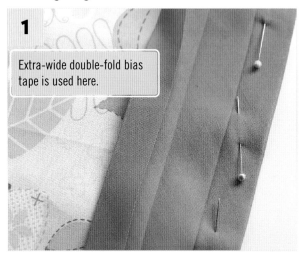

Extra-wide double-fold bias tape is used here.

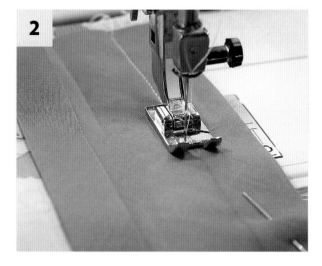

Open the bias tape. Unfold one side all the way, and press it flat. Place the bias tape on the fabric with the right sides together, making sure to line up the raw edges. Pin along the seam allowance.

Straight stitch right along the creased fold line, removing the pins as you sew.

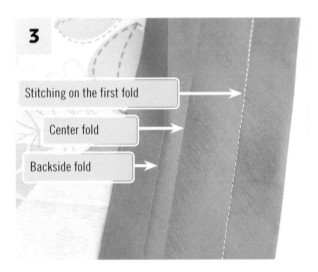

**3**

Stitching on the first fold

Center fold

Backside fold

The straight stitching line is on the first fold. The center fold is just to the left. The part that will fold over to the backside is to the far left.

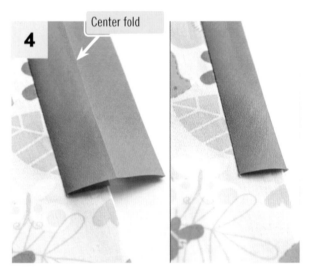

**4**

Center fold

Fold the bias tape over so the center fold lines up with the raw edge of the fabric. Fold the other half to the underside.

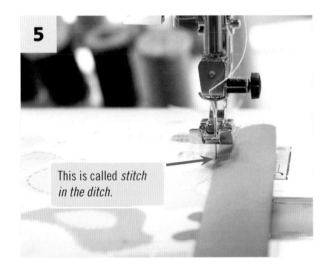

**5**

This is called *stitch in the ditch.*

On the right side of the fabric, straight stitch in the seam where the bias tape joins the fabric. Be sure the part that's folded underneath is caught in the stitching.

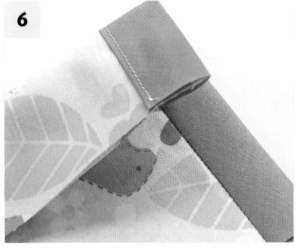

**6**

When you're finished, you will barely see the stitching on the right side. However, notice how it's visible on the backside.

## Sewing a Bias Tape Hem

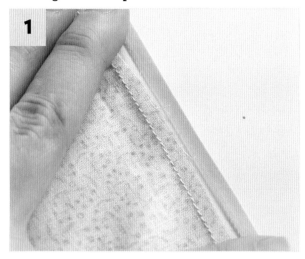

Use a narrow piece of bias tape to finish a hem. Sew it to the right side of the hem line, as in steps 1 through 4 of Binding Edges.

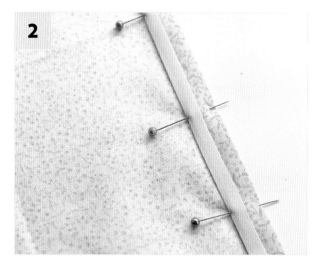

Fold the hem up with the bias tape folded over the raw edge to create an even hem. Pin in place.

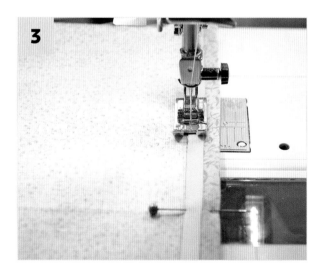

Straight stitch just along the top edge of the bias tape. You can sew an additional parallel line if desired, or sew with a twin needle to create evenly spaced rows.

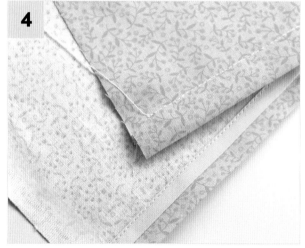

The outside view of the hem shows a single stitching line. The inside view shows a carefully stitched line just at the top edge of the bias tape.

## Mitering a Corner

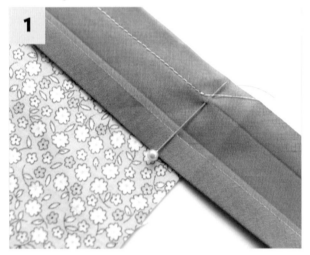

**1**

It's best to miter the corner of a bias tape–trimmed edge. To do this, measure $\frac{1}{4}$ inch (.6 cm) from the edge and mark with a pin. Sew just up to this point.

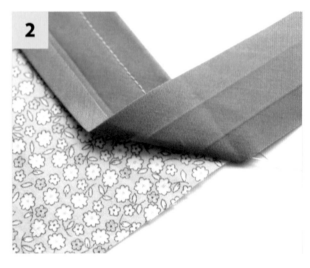

**2**

Fold the bias tape over the sewn part, creating a 45 degree angle from the corner, to keep it lined up.

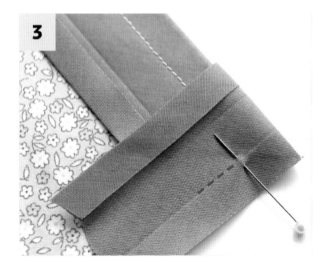

**3**

Fold the bias tape back over to line up with the raw edges on the other side. The folded edge should line up with the adjacent edge. Pin just past the folded fabric underneath.

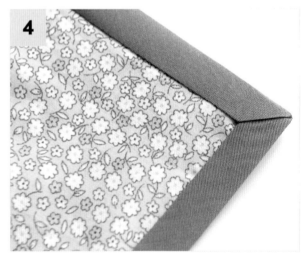

**4**

Turn the bias tape over to fold over the edges and the corner. The backside will have a mitered fold as well.

# Making Your Own Bias Tape

Sure, you can buy prepackaged, prefolded bias tape at the store, but why not make your own? It's pretty simple, and you can choose any color or print you like. Now you can give your projects a truly unique look!

## What You Need

- Cotton fabric
- Plastic or metal ruler
- Fabric marking pen
- Rotary cutter
- Iron
- Scissors
- Bias tape maker tool (optional)

## Binding Edges

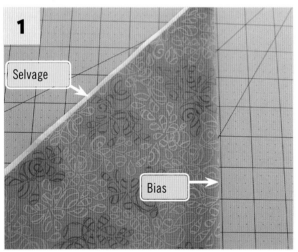

**1**

Selvage

Bias

Fold the fabric with the wrong sides together, so the cut edge lines up with the selvage. Press along the fold to create a crease that runs along the bias of the fabric grain. Open the fabric and lay it flat, with the wrong side up.

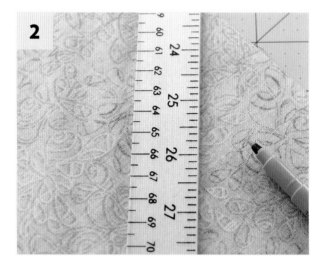

**2**

Create parallel lines at the measurement you want for your bias tape with your fabric marking pen and ruler, using the crease as a starting point (for this example, it is a 2-inch-wide [5 cm] strip).

**3**

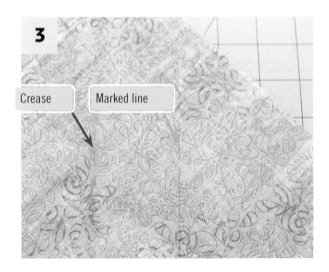

Crease | Marked line

Repeat marking lines across the rest of the fabric on both sides of the center crease.

**4**

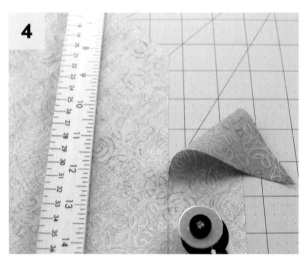

Use a rotary cutter along the edge of your ruler to cut all the strips of fabric.

**5**

Trim the angles off the ends of the fabric pieces to make them square.

**6**

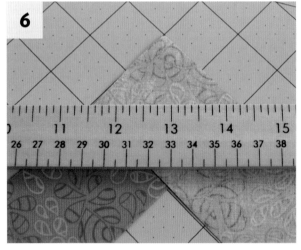

With the right sides together, layer the strips, making sure to match up the right angles. Place the ruler across the corner and line up with the edges of the strips.

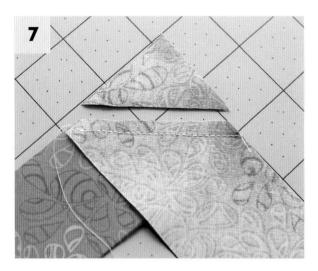

Draw a diagonal line, and straight stitch along the line. Trim the seam to about ¼ inch (.6 cm).

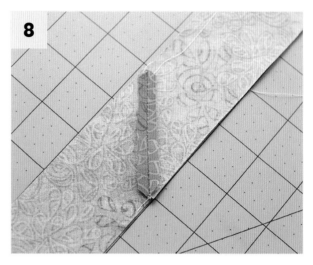

Open up the fabric, and press the seam open. Trim off the edges if they extend past the sides.

The right side of the strip is shown.

The connecting seams will be sewn diagonally across the strip. Continue to sew all the strips together.

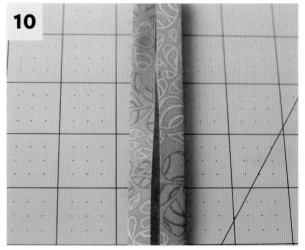

Fold the strip in half, and press it to create the center line. Open and fold the raw edges in toward the center, and press.

## Variation Using a Bias Tape Maker

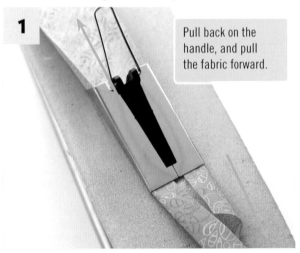

**1** Pull back on the handle, and pull the fabric forward.

Feed the fabric into the bias tape maker tool. As you pull the fabric out, the tool will begin to fold the edges in toward the center.

**2**

As the fabric is pulled out, press it to create creased folds. Once it is all the way out, fold it in half and press the center fold.

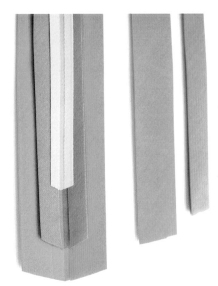

## Types of Bias Tape

Bias tape comes in a variety of sizes designed for different types of projects:

- Single fold simply has the two long edges folded under. Like ribbon, it is stitched along both edges. It comes in two widths and is used for casings, facings, or trim.
- Double fold is similar to single fold but it's folded in half at the center, too. It comes in several widths and is used to finish edges or as drawstring ties that slide into a casing.
- Quilt binding is a larger version of extra-wide double fold. It is used for the edges of quilts or thick blankets.
- Blanket binding has the largest finished size. It's usually made in satin and is just folded in half. It fits right over the edge of a blanket and is straight stitched or zigzagged along the edge.

# Practice Project: Lace-Embellished Tank

## What You Need

- Knowledge of straight seams and attaching trim
- Level of difficulty: Beginner/easy
- Basic, store-bought, camisole-style tank top
- Lace trim of your choice (I've used 44 inches [111.75 cm] of 2 $\frac{1}{2}$-inch-wide [6 cm] tiered lace trim to fit on a size small tank. Simply measure the top edge and around the hem to get the exact dimension needed, and add a few inches for seam allowances.)
- Sewing machine
- Thread
- Straight pins

Add a unique look to a store-bought tank top by simply adding lace trim to the neckline, hem, or both! You can create a bunch of different looks by using different colors, sizes, and types of trims. Make some for yourself or your friends or even to sell.

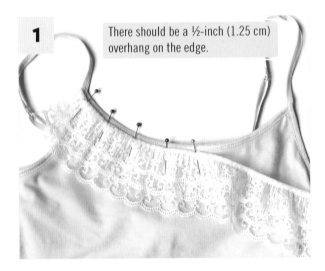

**1**

There should be a ½-inch (1.25 cm) overhang on the edge.

Pin the lace trim to the neck edge of the tank top. Line it up just below the finished edge.

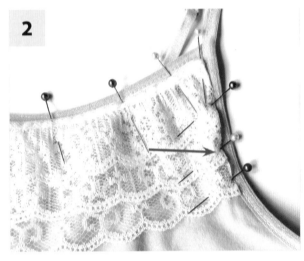

**2**

Fold the edge of the lace under so it fits along the arm edge. Pin it into place, and straight stitch along the top edge and sides.

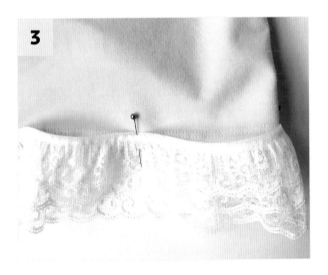

**3**

Start at the side seam and pin the lace to the bottom edge of the tank top. Line it up to cover the existing hem stitching line. Stitch in place just along the top edge. Fold under the overlap at the side seam.

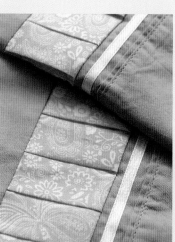

# Part 3
# More Techniques

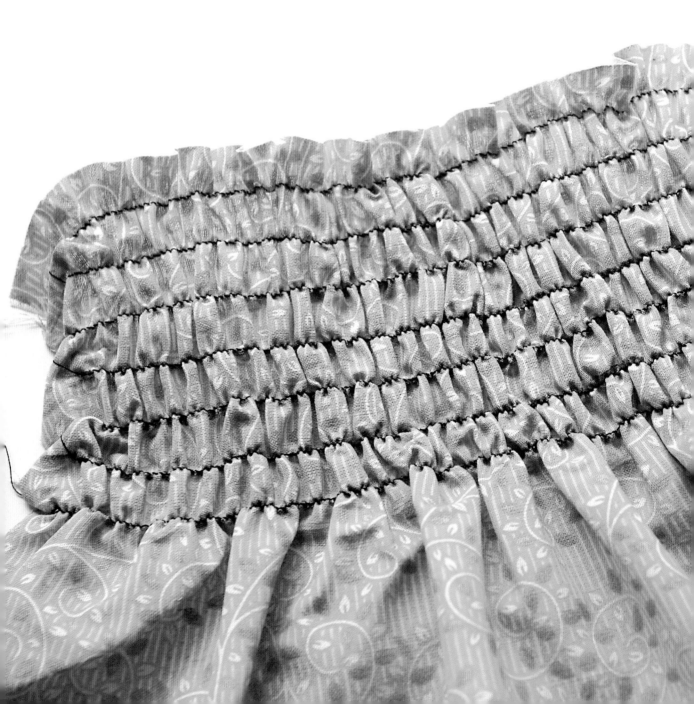

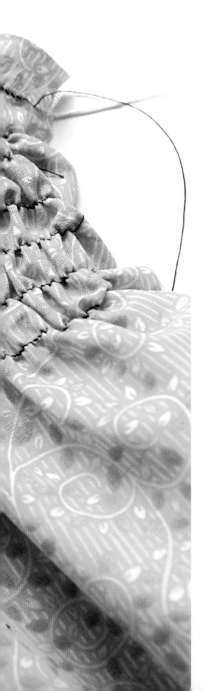

# Chapter 7

## Ruffles and Gathers

# Gathering a Ruffle

From clothes to pillows, ruffles add feminine detail to any project. You can learn to create a ruffle by following these steps.

**1**

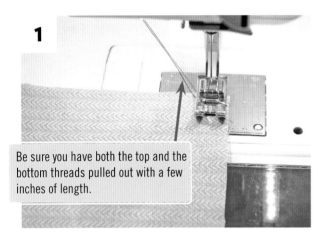

Be sure you have both the top and the bottom threads pulled out with a few inches of length.

Sew a basting stitch at about ¼ inch (.6 cm) from the edge of the fabric. Do not backstitch at either end.

**2**

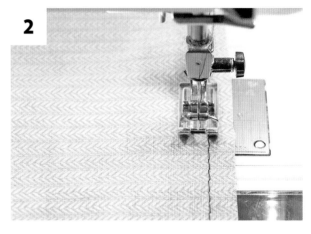

Sew a second row of basting stitches just under the first row at a ³⁄₈-inch (1 cm) seam allowance.

**3**

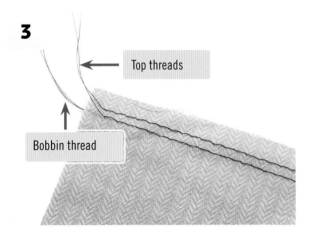

Top threads

Bobbin thread

After the two rows of basting stitches are sewn, separate the top threads from the bobbin thread.

**4**

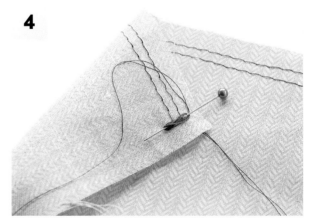

Slide in a pin on the back of the fabric, and wind the bobbin threads around it to secure.

**5**

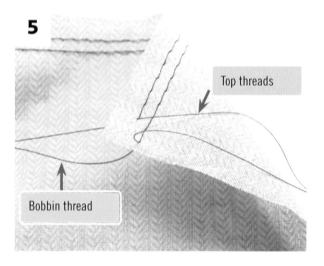

At the other end of the fabric, separate the top threads and the bobbin threads.

**6**

Gently pull the bobbin threads. This will cause the fabric to bunch up.

**7**

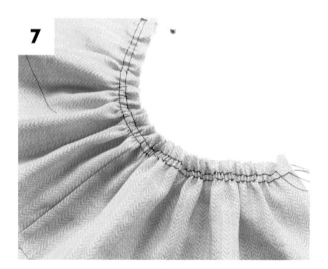

Continue pulling the bobbin threads and sliding the fabric down until you've created the gathered length you desire.

**8**

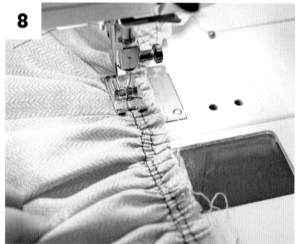

Set the stitch length back to the standard length and carefully sew over the bottom basting line to hold the gathers in place.

# Shirring with Elastic Thread

*What is shirring?* you might ask. It's an old technique that was originally done with regular thread. It features many parallel rows of gathered stitches that create a scrunched-up, gathered look.

A fun and easy way to achieve this look is by doing it with elastic thread. In this example, a skirt waistband is created by sewing lots of straight lines. To begin, wind the elastic thread by hand on an empty bobbin. Then pop the bobbin into your sewing machine as you would regular thread.

## What You Need

- Zigzag (or straight) foot attachment
- Empty bobbin
- Elastic thread
- Ruler and marking pencil
- Spray bottle with water
- Iron

**1**

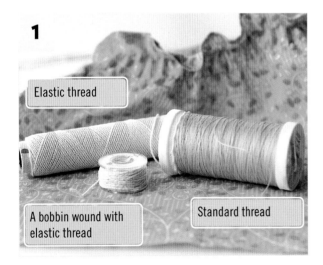

Elastic thread

A bobbin wound with elastic thread

Standard thread

To wind the bobbin, poke the end of the thread through the tiny hole from the inside. Hold the end while winding the thread with a slight stretch.

**2**

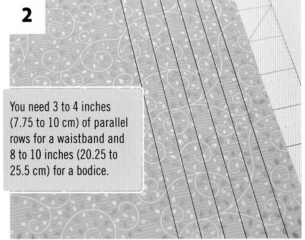

You need 3 to 4 inches (7.75 to 10 cm) of parallel rows for a waistband and 8 to 10 inches (20.25 to 25.5 cm) for a bodice.

Use a ruler and marking pencil to draw straight lines ½ inch (1.25 cm) apart. Create as many rows as you need to get to the desired width.

**3**

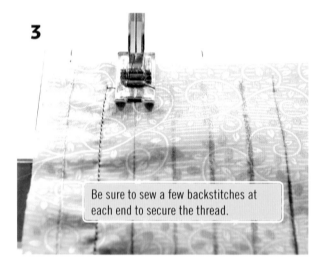

Be sure to sew a few backstitches at each end to secure the thread.

Sew along the lines with a straight stitch. When you get to the end of a row, simply raise the foot and slide the fabric over so you don't have to cut the thread each time.

**4**

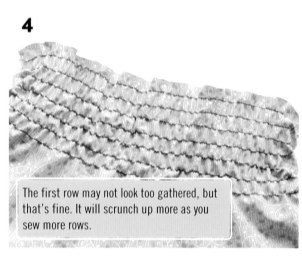

The first row may not look too gathered, but that's fine. It will scrunch up more as you sew more rows.

Continue to sew all the rows of stitching. When you reach the end of the last row, be sure to backstitch to secure the thread.

**5**

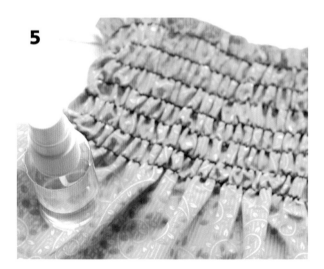

Spray the entire area that is shirred with a mist of water. Press by simply setting the iron on the shirred fabric, picking it up, and setting it on another section (don't slide it around).

**6**

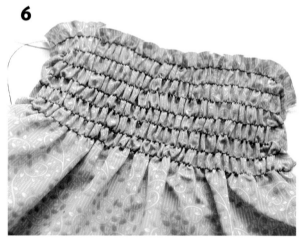

Watch as the elastic magically shrinks! The heat and steam cause the elastic to contract. After it is ironed, the shirred section is nicely gathered up.

# Making Drawstring Ties

Drawstrings can be used in a variety of projects. You can create anything from a cute bag with a simple drawstring closure to a simple apron that ties around the waist. You can make your own tie from fabric, or use a ribbon or rope trim—the possibilities are endless!

Take a glance back at the elastic casing tutorial; this casing will go together the same way. Now, let's focus on how to make a cute drawstring tie! The length of the tie will vary depending on the project.

## What You Need

- Standard foot attachment
- Fat quarter
- Iron
- Safety pin
- Completed elastic casing
- Rotary cutter and ruler

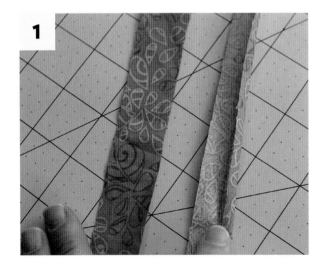

**1**

Using a rotary cutter and ruler, cut two strips of 20 x 1-inch (51×2.5 cm) fabric. Press one strip in half to form a crease at the center. Fold the right outside edge into the center crease.

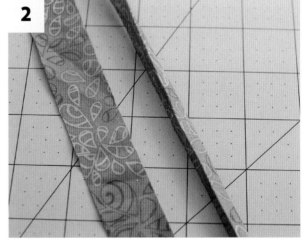

**2**

Repeat this process for the left side of the fabric strip. Press both sides down, and then fold in half so the edges are tucked into the center. Press again.

**3**

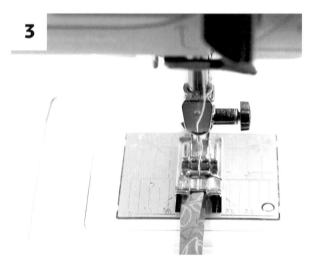

Straight stitch right along the folded edge. Take your time, and keep the seam straight. Your first tie is now complete.

**4**

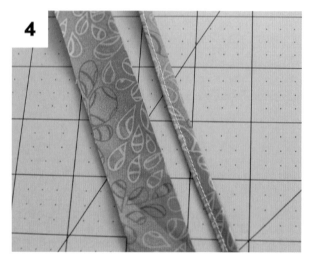

Repeat steps 1 through 3 for the other tie. Most bags will have two ties that pull in opposite directions.

**5**

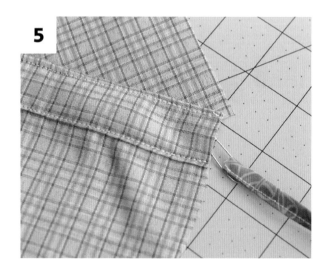

Slide a safety pin into one end of the tie, and use it to feed through the casing. Scrunch up and pull back the fabric until it comes out the other side.

**6**

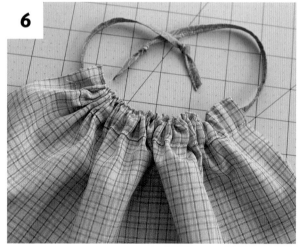

Tie knots on the ends of your ties to keep them from sliding into the casing.

# Sewing with Elastic

Elastic comes in a variety of styles, weights, and sizes. You can use it to create gathers, ruffles, simple waistbands, or straps on a tank top!

Some types of elastic are decorative and exposed, while others are sewn inside casings. You don't need a special machine or special settings to sew with elastic—just your standard presser foot and straight or zigzag stitches. The following lessons will show you a variety of ways to use elastic.

## What You Need

- Zigzag (or standard) foot attachment
- Seam gauge
- Elastic
- Straight pins
- Ruler and marking pencil
- Safety pin

### Elastic Casing

**1**

This example is for ½-inch-wide (1.25 cm) elastic, but you can easily make it any size.

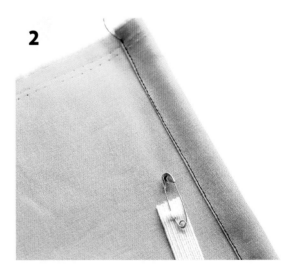

**2**

Similar to the hem, fold the fabric under ¼ inch (.6 cm), press, and fold under again, only this time at ⁵⁄₈ inch (1.5 cm). Pin and sew a straight seam along the inside fold.

Secure a safety pin in the end of the piece of elastic. This will guide it through the casing.

**3**

The casing tube has been created. Notice the hollow space; the elastic will slide into this space.

**4**

Be careful not to squeeze the pin—it might pop open!

Beginning with the safety pin, slide the elastic into the tube. You should be able to gently push the safety pin through the casing.

**5**

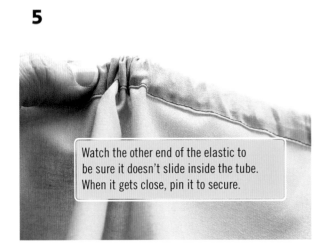

Watch the other end of the elastic to be sure it doesn't slide inside the tube. When it gets close, pin it to secure.

Push the safety pin forward, grip the end of it with your fingers, and slide the fabric back. Keep doing this until the safety pin comes out the other side.

**6**

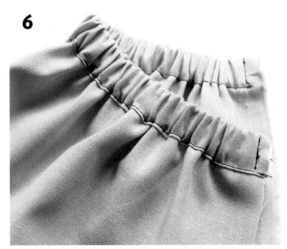

Once you have both ends pulled out of the tube, you can sew a few straight stitches to secure the elastic to the casing on both ends.

## Elastic Ruffle

**1**

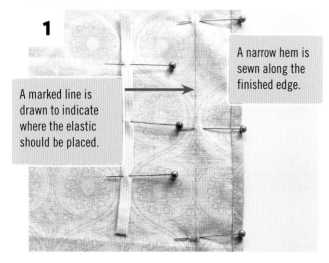

A marked line is drawn to indicate where the elastic should be placed.

A narrow hem is sewn along the finished edge.

Mark the elastic and fabric in fourths with pins—note that the elastic is shorter than the length of the fabric.

**2**

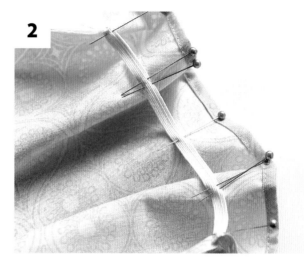

Line up the pins (center to center, fourth to fourth, and so on) and pin the fabric to the elastic at those points.

**3**

Zigzag stitch over the elastic, gently stretching it to the length of the fabric. Carefully sew over the pins, or remove them just before the needle.

**4**

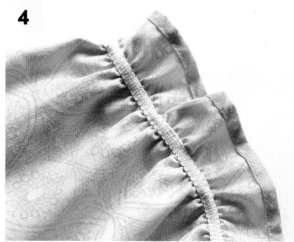

The zigzag stitching secures the elastic to the fabric, creating a ruffle, and stretches with the elastic.

## Exposed Elastic

**1**

Using flat, nonroll elastic, line up the top edge of the fabric so the elastic overlaps about $\frac{3}{8}$ inch (1 cm).

**2**

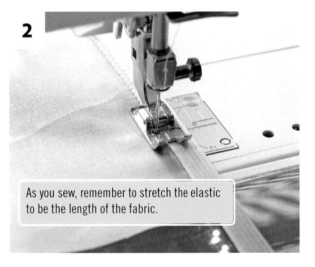

As you sew, remember to stretch the elastic to be the length of the fabric.

Set the stitch to the widest zigzag. Sew along the bottom edge, where the elastic meets the fabric.

**3**

This simple zigzag stitch stretches with the elastic.

# Practice Project: Fabric Headband

Whether functional or a fashion statement, headbands are great to have on hand! This simple tutorial will show you how to create a cute fabric headband with fun, gathered detailing. Choose unique and interesting fabric combinations so you can have a great-looking headband that complements any outfit.

## What You Need

- Knowledge of straight seams and gathering
- Level of difficulty: Beginner/easy
- Two coordinating cotton fabrics (fabric A: 17 x 2$^1/_4$ inches [43×5.75 cm]; fabric B: 34 x 1$^1/_4$ inches [86.5×3 cm])
- 5 x 1-inch (13×2.5 cm) piece elastic (might need to be adjusted shorter for a child-size head)
- Iron
- Straight pins
- Sewing machine

**1**

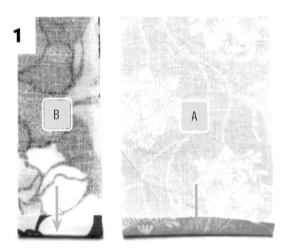

Press the short edges of both fabric A and fabric B under ¼ inch (.6 cm). Sew gathering stitches along both long edges of fabric B.

**2**

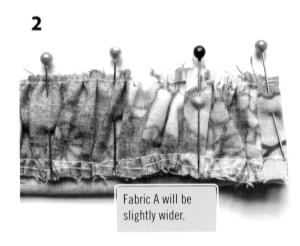

Fabric A will be slightly wider.

Gather fabric B to fit the length of fabric A. With the right sides together, pin the long edges of the two pieces together.

**3**

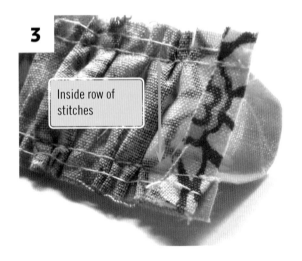

Inside row of stitches

Sew a regular straight stitch along the long edges, just to the inside of the gathering stitches. Backstitch at both ends. Turn the tube right side out.

**4**

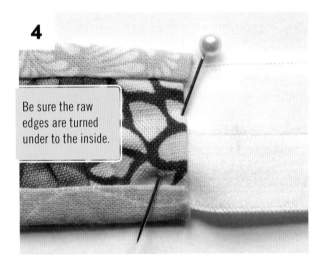

Be sure the raw edges are turned under to the inside.

Press the headband flat. Insert the elastic into the open ends of the headband. Pin, and straight stitch to secure.

# Chapter 8

## Fasteners

Zippers
Buttonholes
Other Fasteners
Practice Project: Zipper Clutch

# Using a Zipper Foot

Don't fear the zipper foot—it's easy to use and can make sewing projects easier! Most sewing machines come with a zipper foot as a standard accessory. If you don't have one, however, just look up your model number to see what's compatible with your machine and order one from your favorite store.

A zipper foot is designed to let you sew right along the edge of something too bulky to fit under a standard sewing foot. There may be specific instructions for some machine models, but the following can help you through the basics of using a zipper foot.

**A zipper foot can be used on more than just zippers...**

- Sew piping trim on an edge or into a seamline.
- Topstitch around a raised fastener, like a snap.
- Sew beaded trim.
- Sew a circular elastic casing.
- Sew in snap tape.

Release the existing foot on your machine; it will drop down and separate from the presser foot holder. Slide it out, and set it aside.

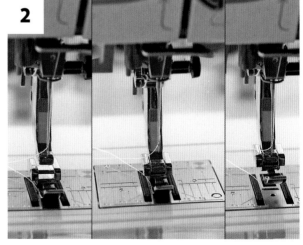

Place the zipper foot under the presser foot holder, lining up the bar directly underneath. Lower the presser foot lever so it latches to the foot, and lift the lever back up.

**3** Notice the needle position—you can't sew with the needle in the center.

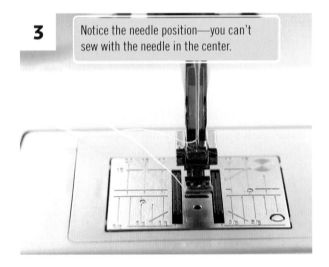

Adjust the needle position so it's all the way to the left or right side of the foot.

**4**

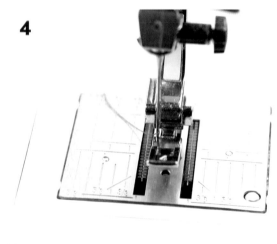

Turn the handwheel slowly to make sure the needle is positioned properly; it should slide down inside the small opening without hitting the foot. Raise the needle back up, and start sewing your zipper.

Separating zipper

Brass jeans zipper

Invisible zipper

All-purpose zipper

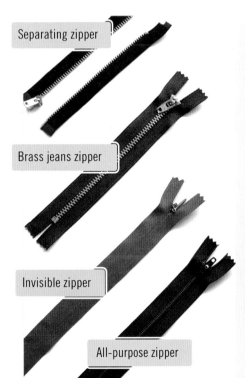

## Shopping for Zipper Types

Zippers come in a variety of styles. The ones you see in the photo are the basics: all-purpose polyester, invisible, brass jeans, and separating.

An all-purpose zipper is exactly what the name implies—it works on all types of fabrics and projects. An invisible zipper is best used with medium or lightweight fabrics and is virtually undetectable when sewn in—all you'll see is the zipper pull. The brass jeans zipper is used in the front fly on denim pants or jeans. Separating zippers are designed to open up all the way. Most often, you'll use these for a jacket or sweatshirt with an open front. Each style can have plastic or metal teeth. Metal teeth are used frequently in an exposed zipper design. Your pattern or project instructions will specify the type you need, so read them carefully to find out the right type to buy.

All zippers can be sewn with a standard zipper foot, but for installing an invisible zipper, it's best to use a concealed zipper foot.

# Inserting a Zipper

Zippers can be both functional and add personality to lots of projects. Don't let a fear of zippers keep you from adding a professional finish to what you're creating!

Sewing a zipper is not difficult at all; it just requires a bit of patience. Try it a few times on scrap fabric, and before you know it, you'll be ready to add one to your next purse or pillow. You can learn many different methods to insert different types of zippers, but for now, here are the basics for inserting a centered coil zipper.

**1**

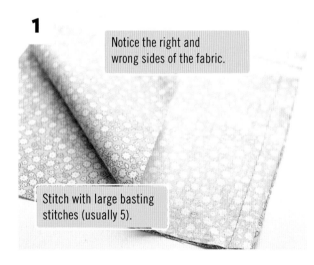

Notice the right and wrong sides of the fabric.

Stitch with large basting stitches (usually 5).

Line up the raw edge of the fabric with the right sides facing each other. Straight stitch ½ inch (1.25 cm) from the fabric edge.

**2**

Use your iron to open the seam and press it flat.

**3**

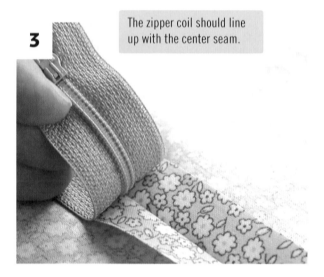

The zipper coil should line up with the center seam.

Place the zipper facedown on the seam. Line up the top edge of the zipper with the top edge of the fabric.

**4**

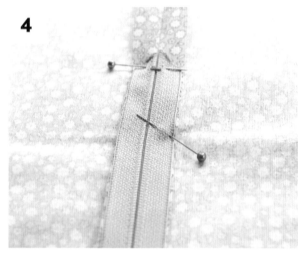

Pin the zipper to the fabric. You can also use a glue stick to hold the zipper in place; just be careful not to get it near the coils and to let it dry before sewing.

**5**

Notice the needle is moved to the far left.

Pull out the pins before sewing.

Lower the zipper foot so it sits next to the zipper coils. Pull out the pin and backstitch a few stitches to secure the seam.

**6**

Don't sew over a pin; you could break your needle.

Continue to straight stitch from the base of the zipper up to the top. Pause with the foot down to remove the pins as you sew.

**7**

Stop sewing 2 inches (5 cm) from the top!

Stop with the needle down. Raise the foot and carefully slide the zipper open so the zipper pull is behind the foot.

**8**

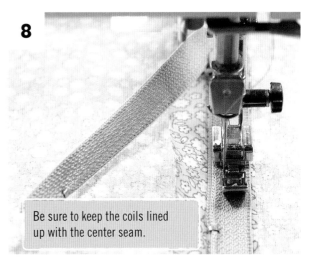

Be sure to keep the coils lined up with the center seam.

Lower the foot and continue stitching to the top edge. Raise the foot and needle, pull the fabric out, and cut the threads.

**9**

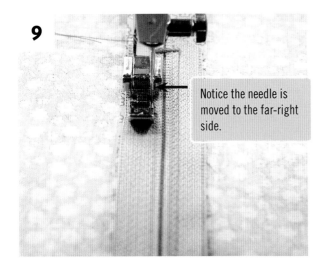

Notice the needle is moved to the far-right side.

Starting at the base of the zipper, sew across the bottom and up the left side. Stop sewing 2 inches (5 cm) from the top edge.

**10**

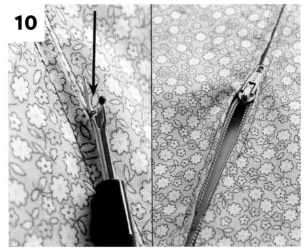

Pull the fabric out of the machine. Use a seam ripper to remove the center basting stitches about 3 inches (7.5 cm) down. Unzip the zipper.

**11**

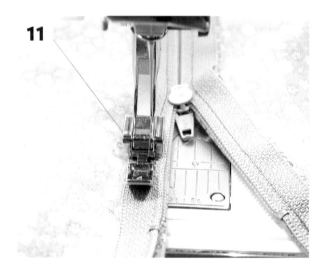

Continue sewing the remainder of the zipper to the top edge. Be sure to keep the coils lined up with the fabric edge.

**12**

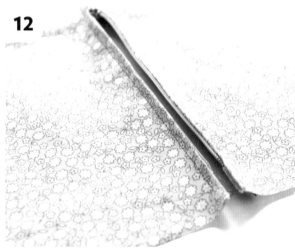

Using the seam ripper, remove the rest of the basting stitches along the center seam. Unzip and zip the zipper to test it.

### It's Easy to Shorten a Zipper to the Perfect Length!

- Place the zipper under the standard sewing foot, or one that works with a zigzag stitch.
- Be sure that the zipper coil is face up and centered under the machine sewing foot. You want the needle to go back and forth over the coil.
- Using your widest zigzag stitch and with your stitch length set to 0, sew several stitches to keep the zipper closed.
- Trim the zipper about 1 inch (2.5 cm) below the stitching. Don't cut through the coils with your fabric scissors—this will damage them! You can use pinking shears or cut at an angle to create a point and prevent fraying.

# Using a Buttonhole Foot

Sewing buttonholes may seem like a scary prospect, but they're not as difficult as they seem. Most sewing machines are equipped with an automatic buttonhole foot, which takes out the guesswork and provides great-looking, consistent results.

An automatic buttonhole can be done in several styles, as you can see in this series of photos.

The following shows you how to use a buttonhole foot to make a simple buttonhole; refer to your machine's manual for the specifics.

## What You Need

- Buttonhole foot attachment
- Button
- Fabric marking pen
- Ruler

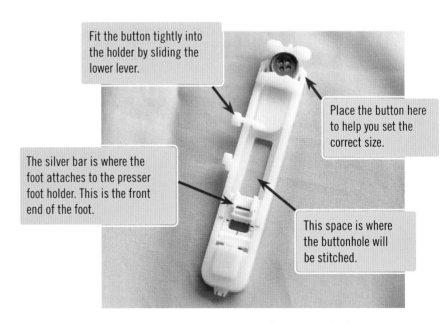

Fit the button tightly into the holder by sliding the lower lever.

Place the button here to help you set the correct size.

The silver bar is where the foot attaches to the presser foot holder. This is the front end of the foot.

This space is where the buttonhole will be stitched.

Study the image to become familiar with the buttonhole foot. Refer to your manual to identify the specific parts.

**1**

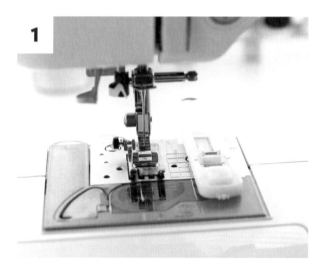

Release the existing foot, slide it out of the way, and set it aside. Position the buttonhole foot under the presser foot holder, and lower it to attach.

**2**

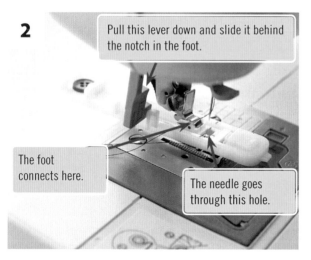

Pull this lever down and slide it behind the notch in the foot.

The foot connects here.

The needle goes through this hole.

Pull down the buttonhole lever and place it behind the notch on the foot. (This works with the button holder at the back of the foot to create the desired-size buttonhole.)

**3**

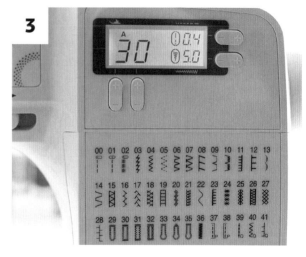

Select the stitch setting for a buttonhole. On this machine, stitch number 30 is selected, and the width and length are set automatically.

**4**

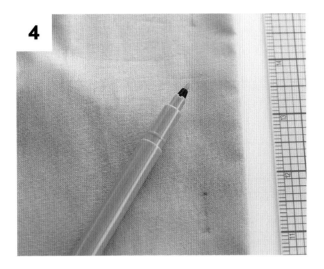

Use a fabric marking pen and a ruler to mark the position of the buttonholes, keeping them at least an inch (2.5 cm) from the edge of the fabric.

**5**

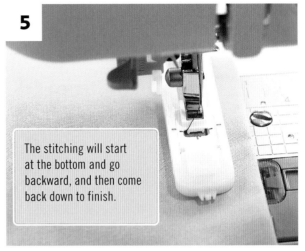

The stitching will start at the bottom and go backward, and then come back down to finish.

Slide the fabric under the foot, and lower the presser foot lever. Line up the bottom edge of the buttonhole mark with the hole in the foot.

**6**

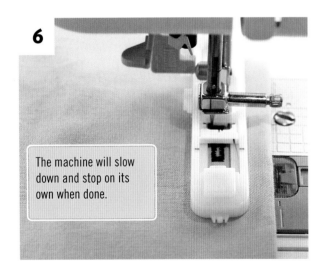

The machine will slow down and stop on its own when done.

Push the foot pedal and let the machine make the buttonhole. The machine will sew up and down a few times on each side, creating a rectangular box with straight stitching. It will then sew a zigzag stitch back and forth over the straight-stitched lines and reinforce with stitches across the bottom and the top.

Keep your hands on the fabric to guide it if necessary, but don't push or pull—let the machine do what it's supposed to do.

**7**

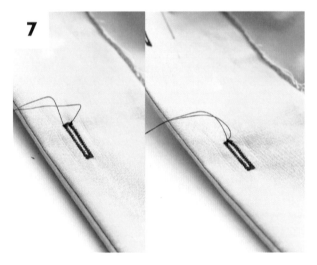

Raise the presser foot, pull out the fabric, and cut the threads. Turn the fabric over to the wrong side. Pull the tail of the top thread through to the bottom, and tie it in a knot to secure. Trim the threads.

**8**

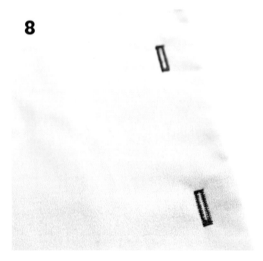

For this buttonhole stitching, you can see the tiny zigzag stitching over the straight stitching on each side. The ends are also strongly reinforced.

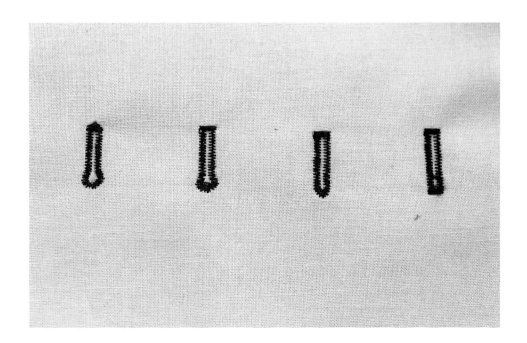

# Opening a Buttonhole

You've created a perfect buttonhole—now it's time to open it up so it's functional! The tiny space that needs to be cut might seem a bit intimidating, but don't worry—I've got a few tricks to share.

Buttons can be used simply as an embellishment or serve a purely functional purpose—and sometimes they can do both. So be on the lookout for interesting buttons!

## What You Need

- Straight pins
- Small, sharp scissors
- Seam ripper
- Seam sealant liquid (such as Fray Check)

**1**

Small embroidery scissors cut easily in tiny spaces!

Place a pin at the end of the buttonhole. This will act as a stop for the tip of the scissors.

**2**

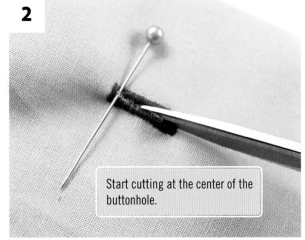

Start cutting at the center of the buttonhole.

Carefully cut forward to the pin at the end. Place a pin at the other end and cut to that end.

**3**

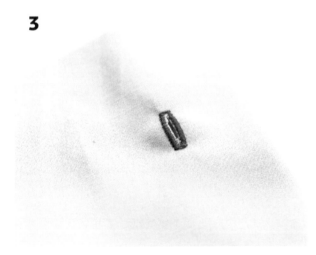

Pull the buttonhole open. Trim any loose threads from the fabric.

**4**

For extra durability, apply the seam sealant liquid to the cut edges. Test it out by sliding a button through the hole.

## Who Knew There Were So Many Types of Buttons?

Buttons are made in a variety of materials, including metal, glass, plastic, clay, ivory, and wood. They vary in shape and size. There are round, oval, square, and even novelty shapes, such as stars and flowers!

Flat buttons can have either two or four holes in the center and can be sewn by hand or sometimes by machine. Shank buttons attach by sewing through a loop under the bottom side of the button.

Choosing the right button is really determined by the overall goal you have for the project. Is the button functional or decorative? It's up to you!

# Sewing a Button

## By Hand

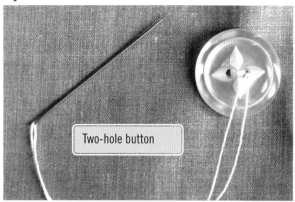

Two-hole button

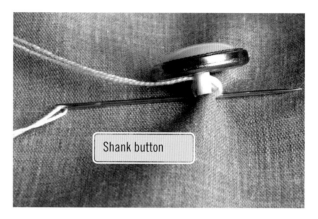

Shank button

For a two-hole button, thread your needle with the thread folded over and tied in a knot to create a double strand. Poke up from the backside through the right hole, and poke back down through the left hole through to the backside—do this three times. Secure with a knot.

To sew a shank button, thread the needle in the same manner as for the two-hole button. Sew up from the backside through the hole and back down to the backside—do this three times. Secure with a tiny knot.

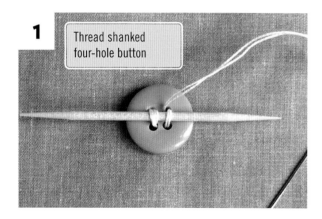

**1** Thread shanked four-hole button

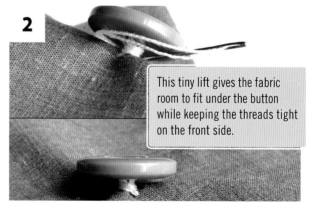

**2** This tiny lift gives the fabric room to fit under the button while keeping the threads tight on the front side.

For extra durability, sew in the same method as for a two-hole button, but sew over a toothpick to create a bit of slack on the thread. Sew the right side followed by the left side—do each side three times. Remove the toothpick.

Poke the needle back up from the bottom, but keep it under the button. Wrap the threads tightly three or four times, and poke back through to the backside. Secure with a tiny knot.

## With a Sewing Machine

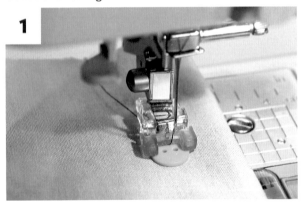

**1**

Place the button foot on the machine. Lower the feed dogs so the fabric isn't pulled back when you begin sewing. Set the stitch to a zigzag at zero length. Place the button under the foot, and lower the foot to hold the button tight.

**2**

Turn the handwheel on the side of the machine to lower the needle into the first hole. The needle should not hit the button at all.

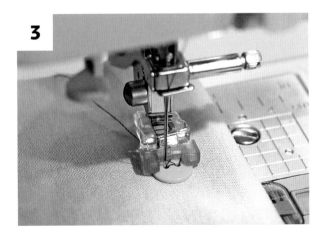

**3**

Continue turning the handwheel to raise the needle and lower it down into the other hole. Make adjustments in the stitch width until the needle can go into both holes without hitting the button.

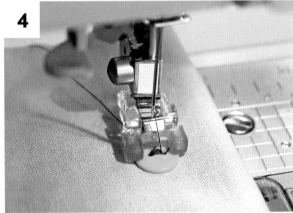

**4**

Sew back and forth several times to hold the button securely in place. Cut the threads, and remove the fabric from the machine. Pull the top thread through to the bottom side and tie it in a knot.

# Sewing with Hooks and Eyes

Commonly used in clothing construction, hook-and-eye closures are small curved metal fasteners with tiny loops that attach to a fabric. A hook and eye is used with seams that meet up. A common place to use them is at the top of a zipper to hold the open edges together.

**1**

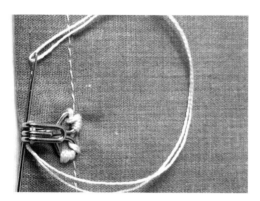

**2**

Position the hook on the underside of the fabric, with the top edge just at the seam edge. Stitch the loops securely a few times, and then come up through the fabric to the top of the hook. Sew a loop or two to secure in place, and secure with a knot.

Sew the eye to the adjacent side about ⅛ inch (.3 cm) from the edge. Sew several times around each loop, being careful to only sew through the top layer of fabric so the stitching isn't visible on the outside.

### Why Choose a Hook and Bar Closure?

- The bar is adjustable and can be moved in or out for a perfect fit.
- It works great for seams that overlap, where a large button would be too bulky.
- A hook and bar is sturdier than a snap; it won't pop open at random!
- It's invisible once closed, giving a clean look to the outside of the garment.

# Snaps and Velcro

Snaps and Velcro have two sides that fasten when pushed together and open when pulled apart. Both are used in the same way on garments, but are sewn on a bit differently.

## Snaps

**1**

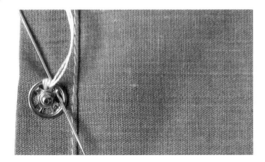

Thread a hand-sewing needle, and tie a knot in the end of the thread. Position the stud side of the snap on the inside edge of the opening. Sew several loops around each of the four holes. Knot the thread again to secure.

**2**

Position the socket side of the snap on the outside of the other side of the opening, making sure it is lined up with the stud side. Sew several looped stitches in each on the four holes, and knot the last stitch to secure.

## Velcro

**1**

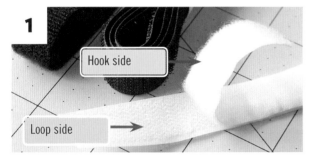

Hook side

Loop side

Velcro has a hook side and a loop side. Cut equal lengths of the desired amount for the opening you are working with.

**2**

Position the pieces so the hook and loop sides will lay on top of each other when the opening is closed. Straight stitch around all four edges to secure, being sure to pivot the corners and backstitch for durability.

# Practice Project:
# Zipper Clutch

This cute little lined wristlet with an exposed zipper is the perfect wallet or makeup bag for when you're on the go. Just add your phone, some cash, your makeup essentials, and the necessary ID and credit cards, zip it up, and you're off!

## What You Need

- Knowledge of straight seams, inserting a zipper, using a buttonhole foot, and sewing on a button

- Level of difficulty: Intermediate

- Cotton fabric in two colors (Fat quarters would work great!)

- 7-inch (17.75 cm) zipper (I used one with large metal teeth.)

- Sewing machine, zipper foot, and buttonhole foot

- Thread

- Scissors

- Straight pins

- Measuring tape

- Iron

- Decorative button

**1**

Purse Fabric
7½ inches (19 cm)

Strap
2½×15 inches
(6.25×38 cm)

Lining Fabric
7½ inches (19 cm)

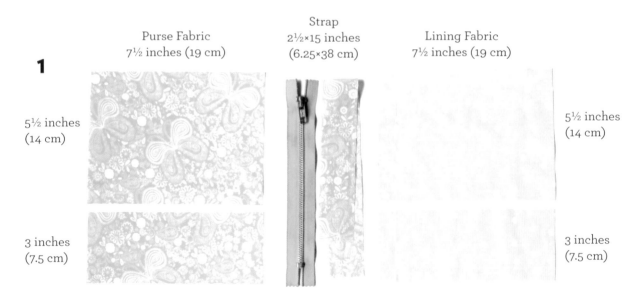

5½ inches
(14 cm)

5½ inches
(14 cm)

3 inches
(7.5 cm)

3 inches
(7.5 cm)

For the purse and lining, cut one 7½×5½-inch (19×14 cm) rectangle and one 7½×3-inch (19×7.5 cm) rectangle. For the strap, cut one 2½×15-inch (6.25×38 cm) strip.

**2**

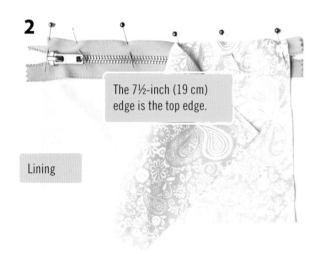

The 7½-inch (19 cm) edge is the top edge.

Lining

Start with the larger rectangle. Place the zipper right side up on top of the right side of the lining fabric. Lay the purse fabric right side down on top of the zipper, and pin through all three layers. Straight stitch about ¼ inch (.6 cm) away from the zipper teeth.

**3**

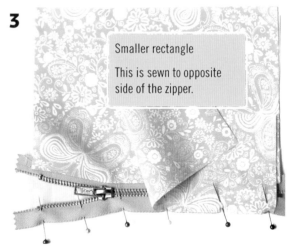

Smaller rectangle

This is sewn to opposite side of the zipper.

Line up the long edge of the smaller rectangle with the other side of the zipper. The right side of the lining piece should go under the zipper, and the right side of the purse fabric should face the right side of the zipper. Pin and stitch ¼ inch (.6 cm) away from the zipper teeth.

**4**

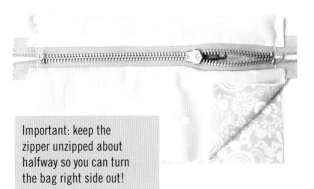

> Important: keep the zipper unzipped about halfway so you can turn the bag right side out!

Fold the fabric open so the purse fabric is face up. Fold the purse in half so the bottom edges line up. The lining fabric should be on the outside. This will create a fold at the top of the purse; the zipper will be about an inch (2.5 cm) down from the top edge.

**5**

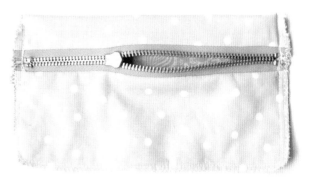

Straight stitch around the sides and the bottom edge. Trim the seams, including zipper ends, to ¼ inch (.6 cm); trim in at an angle at the top corner. Zigzag to finish the seam edge. Turn the purse right side out.

**6**

Press all the edges of the strap under ¼ inch (.6 cm). Press the strip in half lengthwise.

**7**

Topstitch around all the edges, making sure the edges are folded to the inside.

**8**

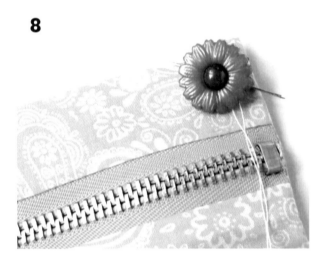

Sew on a button to the top-right corner. (I used a ¾-inch-diameter [2 cm] shank button.) This is how the strap connects to the bag.

**9**

Use your buttonhole foot to create two buttonholes—one at each end of the strap—to fit the button you've selected.

**10**

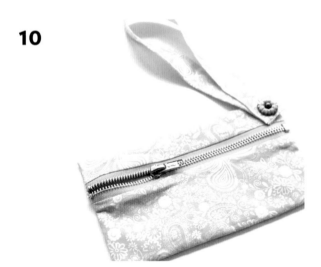

Open the buttonholes up, and slide over the button to create your handle.

# Chapter 9

## Pleats, Tucks, and Darts

Pleats

Tucks

Darts

Practice Project: Pleated Pillowcase

# Knife Pleats

Looking for a great way to add fullness to a piece of clothing or a cute detail to the edge of a pillow? Try knife pleats!

Knife pleats are folds in the fabric that all go in the same direction. Make sure you have the right tools on hand to make evenly spaced straight lines and use a cotton fabric that will hold the crease when pressed. Knife pleats might look intimidating, but don't worry—they're pretty easy to make!

## What You Need

- Ruler
- Fabric marking tool
- Iron
- Straight pins

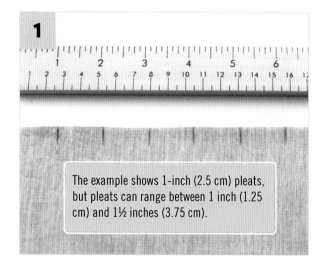

**1**

The example shows 1-inch (2.5 cm) pleats, but pleats can range between 1 inch (1.25 cm) and 1½ inches (3.75 cm).

With the fabric right side up, use a ruler to draw a mark at every inch along the top edge. Three marks will make one pleat.

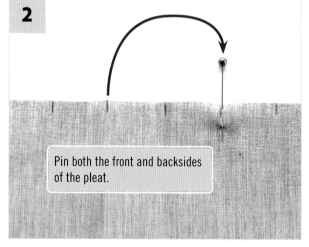

**2**

Pin both the front and backsides of the pleat.

Fold the fabric so the second mark is lined up with the fourth mark. The third mark becomes the inside fold. Pin in place.

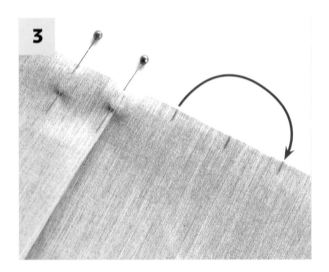

**3**

Take the next set of three marks and repeat the folding process. Continue to pleat the entire length of the fabric, pinning and creasing with your fingers to hold in place.

**4**

Be sure to avoid ironing over the pin heads; they might melt!

Carefully press all the pleats in place, creating crisp, even folds.

**5**

Don't let the fabric fold under the foot!

Use a large basting stitch and sew along the top edge to hold all the pleats in place. Remove the pins as you sew.

**6**

With the basting stitches in place, you can now use the pleats in your sewing project.

# Box Pleats

This type of pleat is a bit more complicated than a basic knife pleat but adds a lot of interest to a project. It can be used as a single pleat (like on the back of a shirt) or in a continuing series (like on a skirt).

Box pleats are made from two folds in the fabric that face away from each other. When done in reverse, with the fabric flipped over, you create an inverted pleat. Both styles are a great addition to your growing skill set!

## What You Need

- Ruler
- Fabric marking tool
- Iron
- Straight pins

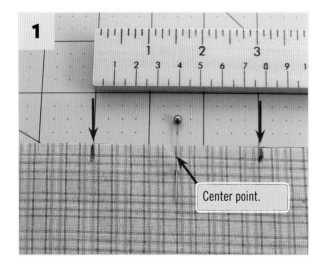

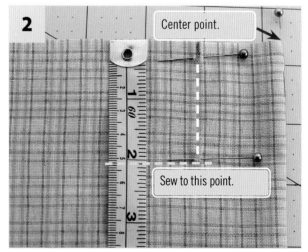

For a single centered pleat: Mark the center point with a pin. Use a ruler to mark a 3-inch (7.5 cm) section, with the pin at the center.

Pinch the fabric at the pin and fold the right side under so the two marks line up. Straight stitch from the mark down 2 inches (5 cm) and backstitch.

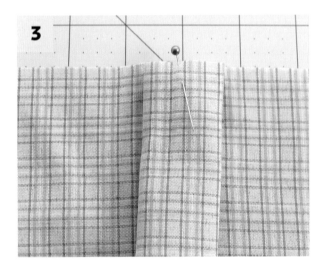

Remove the pins. Open the fabric so the pleat is facing up, and line up the center with the sewn line underneath.

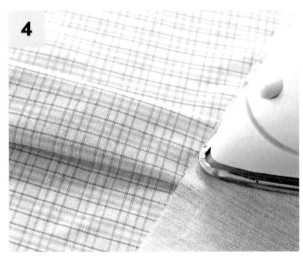

Press the pleat, making sure it is centered and all the way open. Use a thin cloth to protect the fabric if necessary.

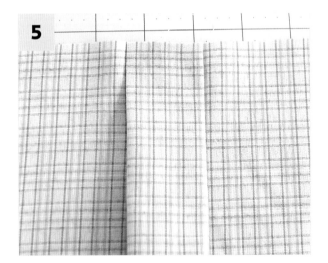

Sew across the top edge with a basting stitch to keep the pleat flat.

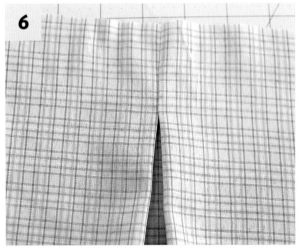

Here is a back view of the finished pleat. This is also called an *inverted pleat* and can be done so this is the finished side.

# Tucks

Both functional and decorative, tucks can add a bit of interest to an otherwise plain-looking project. These long, narrow folds can be used to accent a pillow, add a design element to the bottom edge of a skirt, or make the classic pin tuck–style tuxedo shirt!

It's easiest to use a thin, crisp fabric that will hold a crease when pressed, since this technique is done by following the guide of lots of pressed folds. Stitching a straight line is all you need to know to create this rather complicated-looking design.

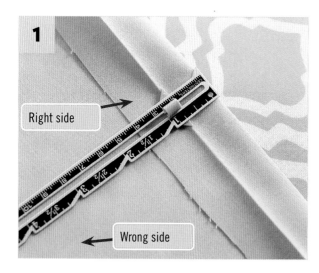

Press a line ¾ inch (2 cm) from the edge of the fabric. Slide the fabric back to measure ¾ inch (2 cm) again.

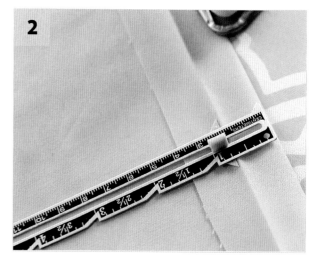

Using the tip or edge of the iron, press the fold down the length of the fabric, creating a crisp crease.

**3**

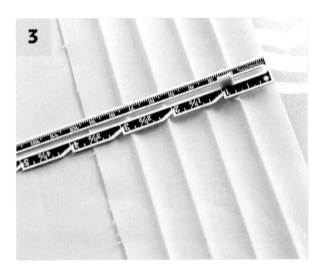

Continue to slide the fabric to the left, and press every ¾ inch (2 cm). Do this for as many tucks as you'd like to create.

**4**

Notice the raw edge of the fabric and the first tuck are sewn.

Sew a straight stitch down the length of each fold using a ⅛-inch (.3 cm) seam allowance from the fold edge. Use the inside of the foot as a guide.

**5**

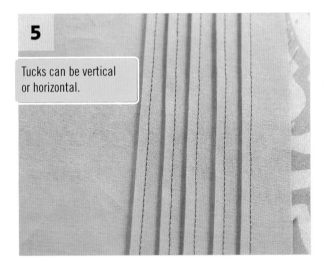

Tucks can be vertical or horizontal.

After all the rows are sewn, press all the folds to one side.

**6**

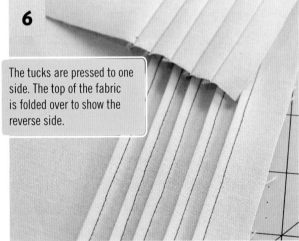

The tucks are pressed to one side. The top of the fabric is folded over to show the reverse side.

Your tucks are now complete and ready to be used in your sewing project.

# Darts

Darts are sort of like angled pleats. They help add the perfect shape to shirts, jackets, and dresses. If you've got something that doesn't fit quite right, you just might need to add a dart or adjust one that's already there. You'll be amazed at the difference a good dart can make to the overall look!

## What You Need

- Ruler
- Fabric marking tool
- Iron
- Straight pins

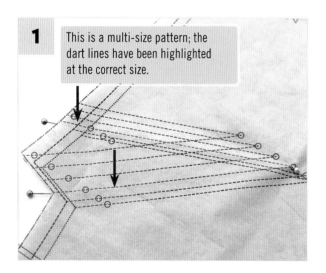

**1** This is a multi-size pattern; the dart lines have been highlighted at the correct size.

Mark the three points of the dart with pins. The pink pin is poked through the tissue pattern.

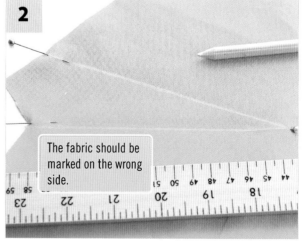

**2** The fabric should be marked on the wrong side.

Use your ruler and fabric marking tool to draw lines from the two side pins to the center point. This creates a slender triangle.

**3**

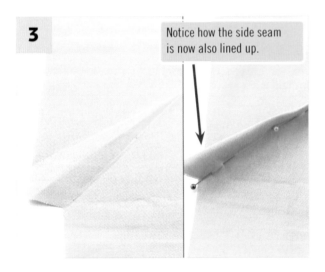

Notice how the side seam is now also lined up.

Fold up the fabric so the drawn lines are lined up. The point will be the end of the fold. Use straight pins to poke through both layers to see whether the markings are lined up exactly.

**4**

With the top side folded under, stitch a straight line on the drawn line, removing the pins as you sew. The angled line will end at the point with one backstitch.

**5**

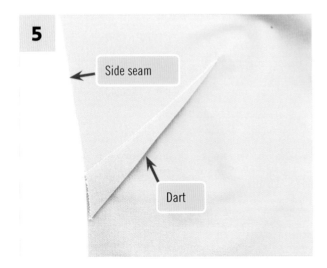

Side seam

Dart

Open the piece back up, and press the dart down toward the bottom of the shirt. Flip over, and press carefully at the point.

**6**

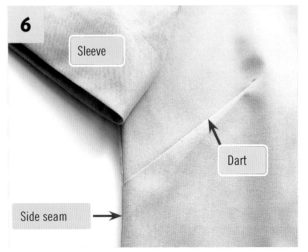

Sleeve

Dart

Side seam

Turn the fabric over to the right side, and use the tip of the iron to press the dart line. Be sure the point makes a smooth transition to the flat fabric.

# Practice Project:
# Pleated Pillowcase

Create your own unique bedding by personalizing a plain pillowcase! Adding a simple pleated strip of fabric and a ribbon embellishment are quick and easy ways to freshen up the look of your bedding. This is a great project for someone just learning to sew—just a few basic sewing skills are required, and everything comes together pretty quickly!

## What You Need

- Knowledge of straight seams, knife pleats, and topstitching trim
- Level of difficulty: Beginner/easy
- Premade or store-bought pillowcase
- 3-inch-wide x 120-inch-long (7.5 x 305 cm) contrasting fabric strip (for a standard-size pillowcase)
- Straight pins
- Measuring tape
- Fabric marking pencil
- Fabric scissors
- $1/4$-inch-wide×21-inch-long (.6 x 53.25 cm) ribbon (or trim of your choice)
- $1/4$-inch-wide (.6 cm) fusible web (such as Steam-A-Seam)
- Iron

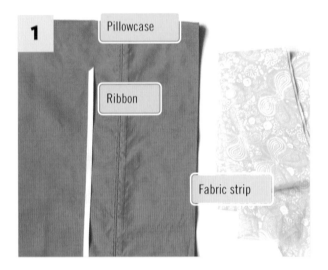

**1** Pillowcase · Ribbon · Fabric strip

Measure and cut out the strip of fabric. You can sew shorter pieces together to make one long strip if desired.

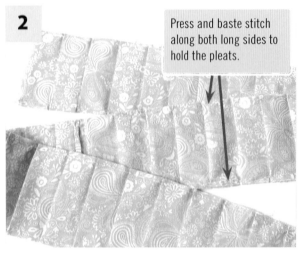

**2** Press and baste stitch along both long sides to hold the pleats.

Pleat the strip using the knife pleat method, forming 1-inch (2.5 cm) pleats pleats along the entire length. With the right sides together, sew the short ends of the strip together to form a loop.

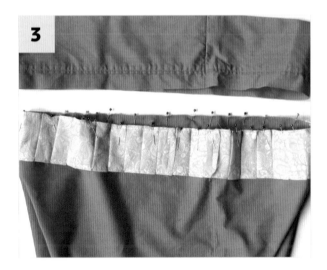

**3**

Measure 5 inches (12.75 cm) in from the open end of the pillowcase, mark it, and cut it off. With the right sides together, pin the pleated strip to the open edge of the pillowcase.

**4** Finish off the edges of the seams with a zigzag stitch to prevent fraying.

With the right sides together, line up the raw edges of the other side of the pleated strip with the cut-off portion of the pillowcase, and sew them together. Press so both seams point away from the opening.

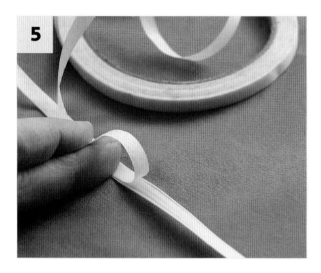

Use your fingers to press the textured, sticky side of the fusible web onto the backside of the ribbon.

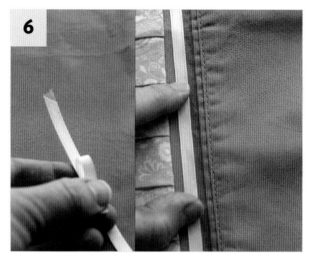

Peel off the paper backing and firmly place the ribbon, sticky side down, in the space between the pleats and the stitching line of the pillowcase.

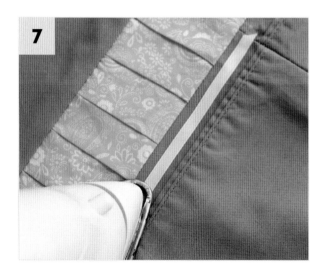

Press a section of the ribbon with a hot iron to heat up the glue and fuse it to the pillowcase—5 seconds under the iron is enough time. Pick up and press the next section until all the ribbon has been pressed. Fold under the cut end at the overlap.

**8**

Even though the ribbon is fused, for extra durability, topstitch along both outside edges of the ribbon. Slide your pillow inside, and you're finished!

# Chapter 10

## Decorative Techniques

# Applying Appliqué

You can learn to do a variety of styles of appliqué—raw edge, satin stitched, double layer, and reverse appliqué, to name a few. Appliqué can be used to add pop or a unique flair to a project or to even patch a tear or hole.

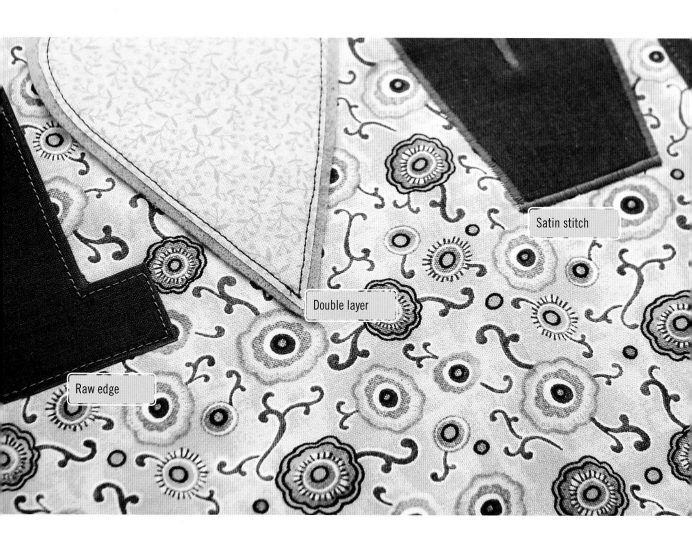

Satin stitch

Double layer

Raw edge

## Basic Appliqué

Here, I show you how to sew an appliqué—something you'll be using for years to come!

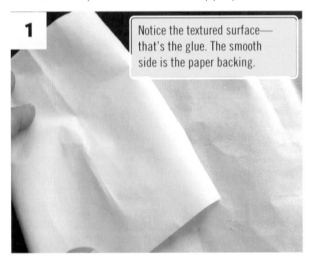

**1**

Notice the textured surface—that's the glue. The smooth side is the paper backing.

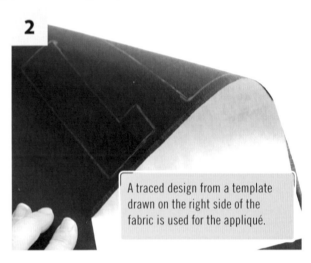

**2**

A traced design from a template drawn on the right side of the fabric is used for the appliqué.

Make sure you have fusible web, such as Heat and Bond or Wonder Under—it's necessary to do the appliqué. You can find fusible web in sheets or a roll.

Cut a piece of the fusible web large enough to cover the area of the appliqué design. Iron it to the wrong side of the fabric, textured side down. Cover the fusible web with a pressing cloth to protect it and the surface of the iron.

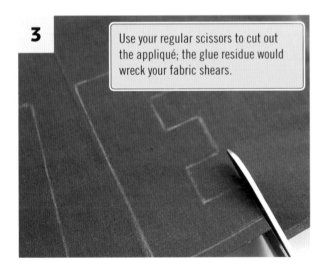

**3**

Use your regular scissors to cut out the appliqué; the glue residue would wreck your fabric shears.

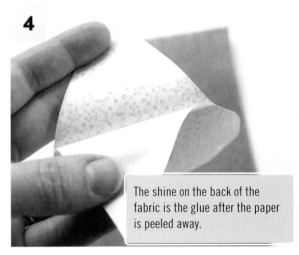

**4**

The shine on the back of the fabric is the glue after the paper is peeled away.

Let it cool. Cut out the design, making sure to cut through the fabric and the paper backing.

Carefully peel off the paper backing. You should see the backside of the design covered with a clear, shiny sheet.

**5**

Position the design on your fabric, and press with a hot iron to heat up the glue backing and fuse it to the fabric. Once it cools, stitch around the edge with your desired stitch.

**6**

The first layer has been pressed and straight stitched just inside the raw edge.

To create a double-layer appliqué, simply press and stitch the first layer to another piece of fabric. Trim around the edges, and apply the fusible web to the back to apply it to the project.

### Making Appliqué

You can make an appliqué from any printed fabric. Simply iron the fusible web to the backside of the fabric, large enough to cover the design.

Then, cut out the shape or graphic, peel off the backing paper, and apply it to whatever you desire. It can go on anything from a t-shirt, to a bag, to a pillow!

## Using Reverse Appliqué to Fix a Tear

Reverse appliqué is done by cutting out the desired shape from the main fabric and revealing the appliqué fabric underneath the open area. It's also a quick, easy, and cute way to fix a hole in something you wear, such as jeans.

Cut a piece of fabric slightly larger than the tear or hole.

Place strips of the Steam-A-Seam product, sticky side down, around the edges of the right side of the fabric. Press down with your fingers so it sticks to the fabric. Peel off the paper backing, being sure the glue is left on the fabric.

Slide the fabric right side up into the pants leg so the fabric fills the hole and the sticky edges are around the perimeter of the hole. Press with an iron to heat up the glue and fuse the two fabrics together.

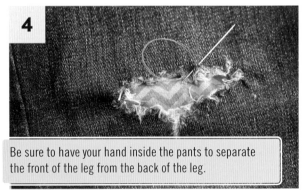

Thread a hand-sewing needle with thread or embroidery floss. Stitch tiny, decorative stitches around the edges of the pants hole. Secure the thread with a small knot to finish the patch.

# Practice Project:
# Monogrammed Key Fob

Adding a stylish key fob is a great way to personalize a set of keys. You can make key fobs in a variety of shapes and sizes, so have fun with fabrics and your choice of appliqué. Make one for yourself or even a friend!

## What You Need

- Knowledge of curved seams, appliqués, and quilting
- Level of difficulty: Beginner/easy
- Two coordinating cotton fabrics, cut into small circles of the same size (1 ¾ inches [4.5 cm] in this example)
- Small piece felt for center layer, cut into the same-size circle
- Lightweight fusible interfacing (such as Wonder-Under)
- Key ring
- 2-inch-long (5 cm) twill tape *or* ½-inch-wide (1.25 cm) ribbon

**1**

The interfacing is applied on wrong side of the fabrics.

Cut out and apply fusible interfacing to the back-sides of the two cotton fabrics. Add the appliqué to the top layer.

**2**

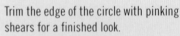

Trim the edge of the circle with pinking shears for a finished look.

Layer the three circles with the felt in the center and the right sides facing out. Stitch around the edge of the circle, leaving a small opening at the top.

**3**

Fold the twill tape over the key ring, and slide the raw edges into the opening in the fabric between the fabric layers. Pin and stitch the remainder of the circle.

# Types of Quilting

Quilting is a technique where you layer three fabrics to create a thicker, padded material. It is often used to create quilts, but it can also be used to create pot holders, placemats, or even pillow covers. It's possible to quilt using your standard sewing machine foot when working on small projects with no intersecting lines. As you advance in this area and move on to bigger projects, however, you'll likely want to invest in a quilting foot, walking foot, or free-motion foot.

The different quilting methods are shown here—follow along and practice with small scraps to perfect the technique. You'll be making cute, quilted projects in no time!

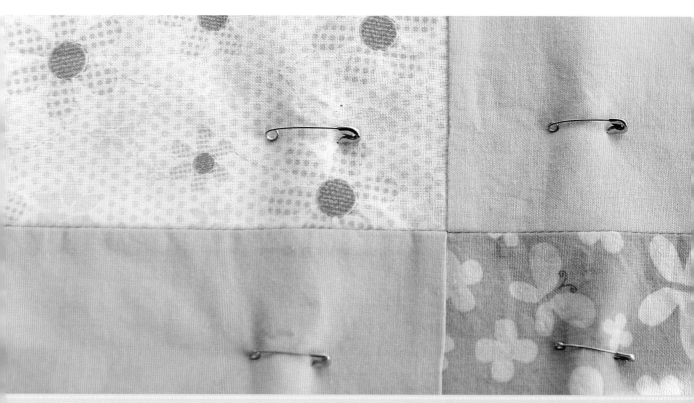

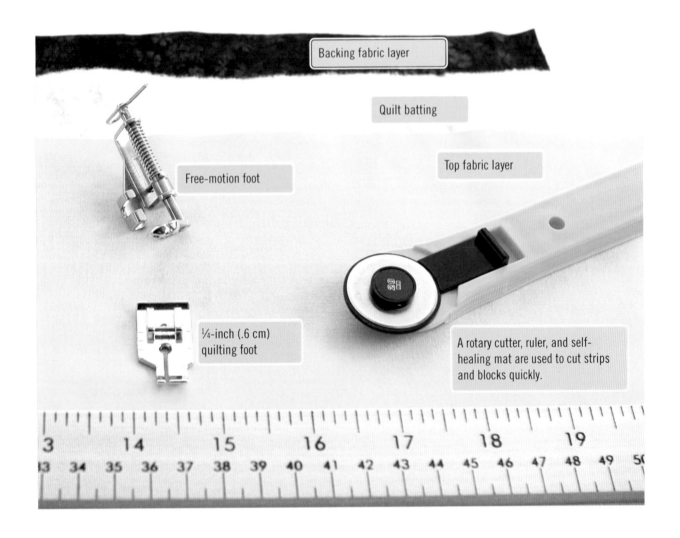

Backing fabric layer

Quilt batting

Free-motion foot

Top fabric layer

¼-inch (.6 cm) quilting foot

A rotary cutter, ruler, and self-healing mat are used to cut strips and blocks quickly.

**Note:** Most quilted projects are finished off with quilt binding that wraps around the layered raw edges. You can buy it prepackaged or make your own in a variety of widths.

## Channel and Diamond Quilting

Channel quilting has evenly spaced, straight lines. The lines can be horizontal, vertical, or diagonal.

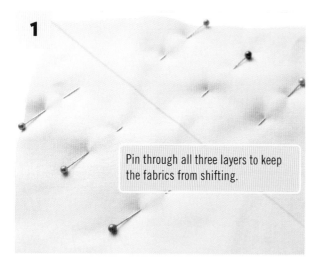

**1**

Pin through all three layers to keep the fabrics from shifting.

Layer the three fabrics, with the quilt batting between the top and backing layers, right side facing out. Starting at the center, mark your stitching line on the top layer.

**2**

The pins are placed around the machine foot; it's best to leave them in while sewing.

Following your marked line, straight stitch through all three layers. Keep the fabric layers sandwiched together and guide them through as one unit.

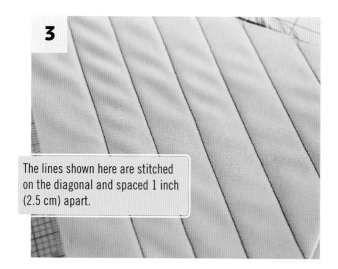

**3**

The lines shown here are stitched on the diagonal and spaced 1 inch (2.5 cm) apart.

Measure and mark the remaining lines. Continue to straight stitch along all of the evenly spaced marked lines. Remove the pen marks with a light mist of water.

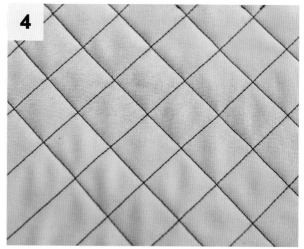

**4**

Draw lines that intersect with your first set of diagonal lines to create a diamond pattern, and pin to prevent the fabric from puckering. Straight stitch along all of the marked lines.

## Stitch in the Ditch Quilting

Stitch in the ditch quilting draws attention to the pieced design because it follows the seam lines.

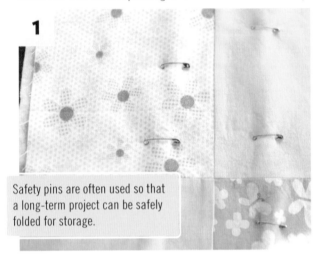

**1**

Safety pins are often used so that a long-term project can be safely folded for storage.

Layer the pieced design at the top of your quilt stack. Pin through all three layers, leaving space for the machine foot to sew without having to remove the pins.

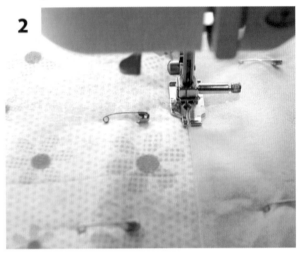

**2**

Sew a straight stitch right into the well of the seam. Keep the fabric tight, and guide it through without letting the layers shift.

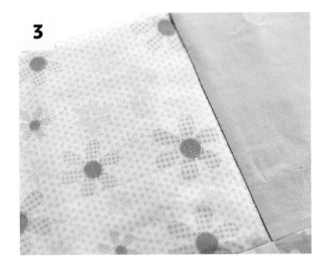

**3**

The stitched line is sewn right into the seam to emphasize the design and have each section stand out. When done with a matching thread, you'll only notice the outlined shape.

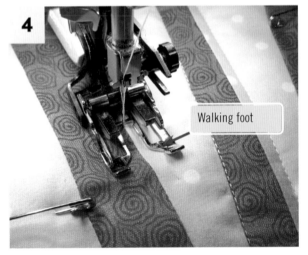

**4**

Walking foot

A walking foot has a set of feed dogs on the bottom of the foot. This is designed to work with the feed dogs on the machine to pull both layers of fabric together evenly.

## Outline Quilting

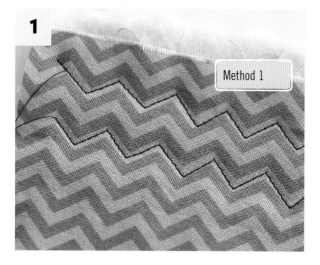

**1** Method 1

**2** Method 2

Stitch along the pattern of the fabric to create an outline design. Pin and stitch, following the same instructions mentioned in step 1 of Channel and Diamond Quilting.

Stitch ¼ inch (.6 cm) away from the pieced seams, pivoting at the corners. Use the ¼-inch quilting foot as a guide to keep the seams consistent.

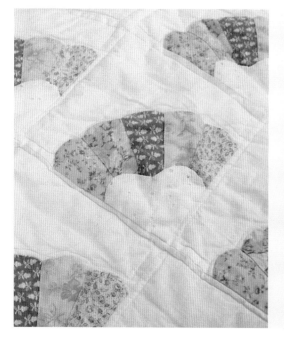

### What Is a Quilt Block?

A quilt block is a small square piece of the top layer of a quilt. It can be pieces of fabric sewn together or an appliquéd design. You can find a variety of patterns for quilt block designs.

Sewing the blocks together will make one quilt top. The blocks for a quilt can be identical or made up of different designs—it's entirely up to you.

Sewing one block at a time makes it very easy to work on a quilt project over a long period of time!

## Free-Motion Quilting

**1**

Free-motion quilting requires a special foot called a *darning foot.*

Remove the current foot and stem with the tool included with your machine. Loosen it just enough to slide the entire piece out.

**2**

Notice the feed dogs are in the up position.

Place the new foot on the screw, and tighten it to secure. Be sure to check the needle position; it needs to line up with the hole in the foot. Refer to the specific instructions for your machine.

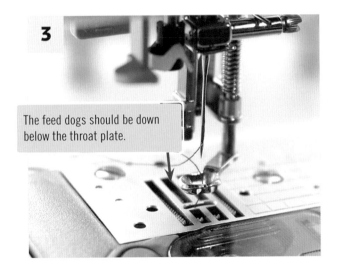

**3**

The feed dogs should be down below the throat plate.

Locate the button or lever and press or pull to lower the feed dogs on your machine. This is a crucial step in the free-motion technique.

**4**

Use both hands to create swirl-type movements. The fabric won't move unless you guide it.

With your machine set to a straight stitch, begin sewing. The fabric will be free to move around to create any random design you choose. Practice this method to perfect it.

# Practice Project: Pot Holder

Interested in the idea of quilting, but feel a bit intimidated at the same time? Make a pot holder! It's a great way to practice basic quilting skills while designing a pretty and functional accessory for your kitchen. You can even piece together scrap fabrics to create a unique patchwork-style design for the top or bottom layer.

## What You Need

- Knowledge of straight seams, quilting, and hand stitching
- Level of difficulty: Beginner/easy
- Two pieces 9-inch (23 cm) square cotton fabric
- Batting
- $2^1/_2 \times 38$-inch ($5.75 \times 96.5$ cm) binding fabric
- Straight pins
- Safety pins
- Iron
- 5-inch (12.75 cm) piece ribbon for loop
- Sewing machine
- Walking foot (optional)

**1**

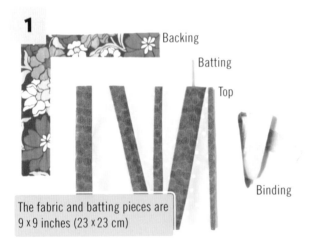

Backing

Batting

Top

Binding

The fabric and batting pieces are 9 x 9 inches (23 x 23 cm)

Gather your pieces. The batting may need up to three layers, depending on the thickness you desire. I created the top piece for this by piecing together strips of fabric before cutting out.

**2**

Layer the three square pieces. Pin them using safety pins or straight pins, making sure to cover most of the area to prevent the pieces from sliding.

**3**

Following the lines of the fabric, quilt along the seam lines, or mirror them by sewing along the line but $1/4$ inch away. Sew around all four edges as well.

**4**

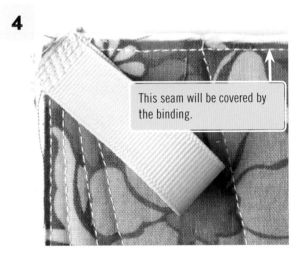

This seam will be covered by the binding.

Fold the ribbon in half lengthwise, and sew to the top corner of the backside of the pot holder.

**5**

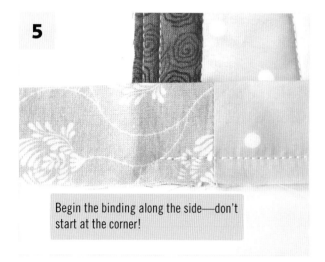

Begin the binding along the side—don't start at the corner!

Fold the binding fabric in half lengthwise, right sides out, and press. With the raw edges lined up, start by placing the binding along one of the sides, and stitch along the edge.

**6**

Fold the binding fabric down to create a diagonal fold pointing in from the corner. Press the fold flat.

**7**

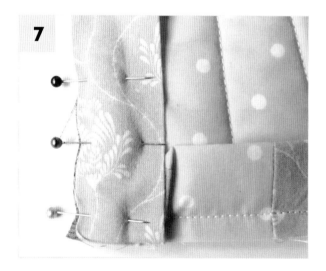

Fold the binding back up to overlap the diagonal fold. Pin, and sew along the side. Repeat for all four corners.

**8**

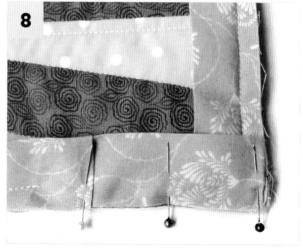

When the binding reaches the starting point, trim any excess length, turn the edge under, and layer over the other raw end. Pin in place, and continue straight stitching the seam.

**9**

Fold the binding over the raw edge of the pot holder. Hand stitch using a whipstitch to sew down the binding to the backside of the pot holder. (You also have the option of doing a top-stitch on your machine.)

# Chapter 11

## Basic Clothing Techniques

# Using Interfacing

## What Is It Used For?

Interfacing is applied to a layer of fabric to add shape, support, structure, or firmness to collars, cuffs, waistbands, and pockets. It is also used to stiffen fabrics used in craft projects, such as purses or fabric boxes.

Interfacing comes in two types: fusible and sew-in. Each type has varying weaves—knit, woven, and nonwoven—and can be light, medium, or heavy in weight. Interfacing is usually found in white/cream or black.

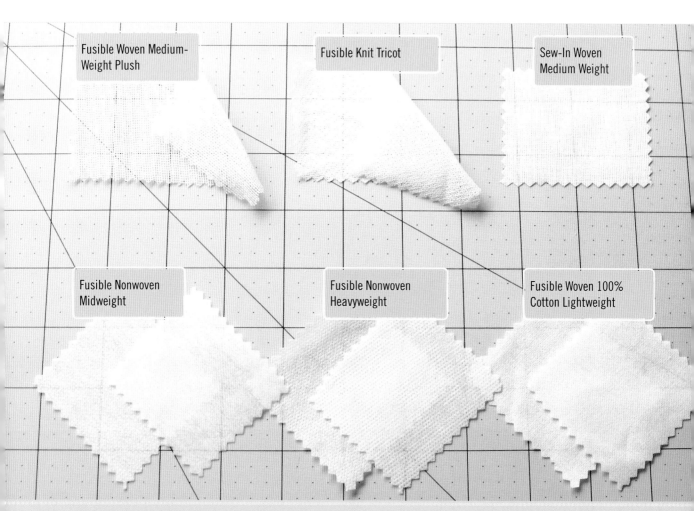

Fusible Woven Medium-Weight Plush

Fusible Knit Tricot

Sew-In Woven Medium Weight

Fusible Nonwoven Midweight

Fusible Nonwoven Heavyweight

Fusible Woven 100% Cotton Lightweight

## How Do You Choose the Right Type?

When you're sewing with a pattern, it will usually specify the type, weave, and weight of interfacing required, so be sure to read the instructions thoroughly.

The weight of sewn-in interfacing should be the same as the fabric—for example, medium-weight fabric would use medium-weight interfacing. The intended use also determines the weight you need—a cuff may need a stiffer interfacing than a floppy-style collar, for instance.

Always choose knit interfacing for knit fabrics. This includes stretch fabrics and jersey knits, where it's necessary to have the interfacing stretch with the fabric.

Nonwoven interfacing is all purpose and can be cut in any direction, so it is the most economical form of interfacing. It can pretty much be used on any woven fabric except for something sheer, like silk.

Like fabric, woven interfacing has a lengthwise and crosswise grain and needs to be cut in the same direction as the fabric it is being used with.

For best results, use dark-colored interfacing with dark fabrics and the white or natural-colored interfacing with light fabrics.

*Fusible interfacing* is the easiest to use and will work with most fabrics. It has a textured side with glue applied to it. It is heat activated, so all you have to do is place the interfacing textured side down on the wrong side of the fabric and press it with a hot iron to heat up the glue and fuse or bond it to the fabric. You shouldn't use fusible interfacing on a fabric that can't be ironed at a high heat or a heavily textured fabric, because it won't stay fused. It also shouldn't be used on something like lace, because the glue will leave a residue on the front side of the fabric.

Read the directions that come with your fusible interfacing; each weight and type will have specific instructions related to heat and the time it takes to bond. Generally, you will press the fusible interfacing in sections by picking up the iron and setting it back down. You won't slide the iron around, because doing so may shift the layers. You'll also want to use a pressing cloth to protect the surface of the iron from any glue residue.

*Sew-in interfacing* is applied by being sewn to the fabric layer and is less commonly used than the fusible type.

# Pockets

Pockets are both functional and decorative. You can have a pocket tee, pants pockets, back pockets, cargo pockets, and even zippered pockets. Every project is unique, and each pocket may have its own set of instructions, so be sure to refer to your pattern or tutorial instructions for specifics.

The pieces used to illustrate the steps here for attaching a pocket were cut out from a purchased pattern. Follow along to see how easy it is to sew a topstitched pocket.

## What You Need

- Cut-out fabric pocket
- Iron
- Fabric marking tool
- Point turner

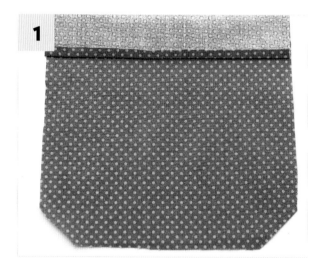

**1**

Press the top edge of the pocket under $1/4$ inch (.6 cm). With the right sides together, press the top edge over 1 inch (2.5 cm).

**2**

Don't stitch across the top.

Straight stitch at a $5/8$-inch (1.5 cm) seam allowance from the top edge on the right side, being sure to keep the folded edge turned up as it goes under the foot.

**3**

Trim seam allowance for folded portion.

Sew down and around the perimeter of the pocket edge. Follow the corners or curved edges, keeping a consistent seam allowance.

**4**

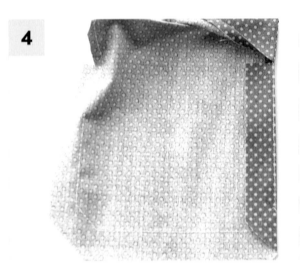

Turn the folded edge right side out. Use a point turner or a pencil to push the corners out to a sharp point.

**5**

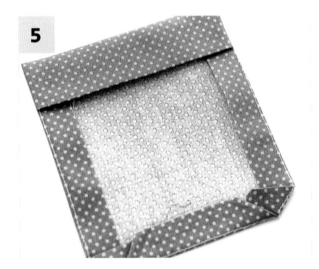

Press the pocket edges under along the stitching line, following the shape of the pocket corners.

**6**

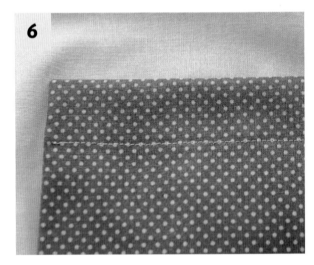

Position the pocket where you'd like it to go, or to line up with the markings on the garment transferred from a pattern.

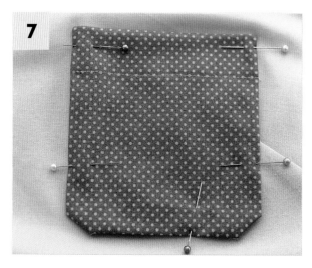

**7**

Pin the outside edges of the pocket, being careful to only go through the pocket and a single layer of fabric.

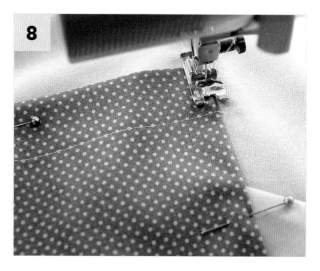

**8**

Sew a straight stitch just along the edge of the pocket. Backstitch at the beginning to reinforce and secure.

**9**

Use the needle-down position to pivot at the corners. Remember to remove the pins as you sew.

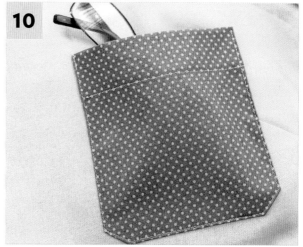

**10**

Backstitch to finish the seam at the top-left side of the pocket. Your pocket is now done and ready to use!

# Attaching a Collar

## What You Need

- Standard foot attachment
- Scissors
- Iron
- Straight pins
- Point turner or pencil

The most common way to finish a neck opening is by attaching a collar. The simplest type of collar to attach is a convertible collar, which is sewn directly to the neckline of the shirt without a collar stand and lined with a simple facing to give it a clean, finished look.

You should read and follow your pattern instructions to know the exact method for your specific project, but on the next few pages, I show you the basic idea for attaching a collar using a simple shirt design and a basic pointed collar.

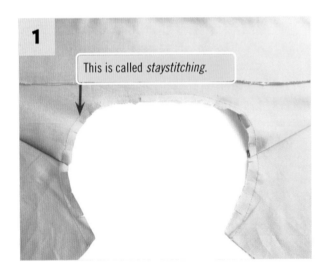

Sew the shoulder seams and stitch a straight stitch around the neck opening. Sew the collar and turn it right side out. Use an iron to press the collar and shoulder seams open.

Snip into the seam allowance just up to the stitching line.

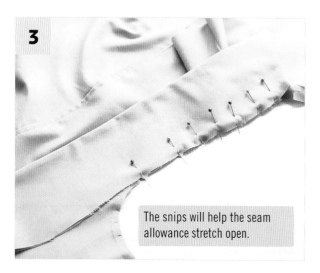

**3**

The snips will help the seam allowance stretch open.

With the notches lined up, pin the collar to the shirt. Start at the center in back and work your way to the front.

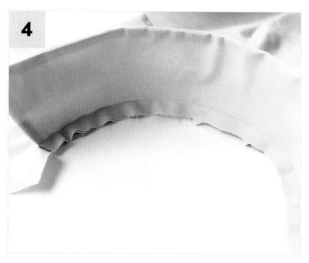

**4**

Using a basting stitch, sew a straight stitch along the edge of the collar.

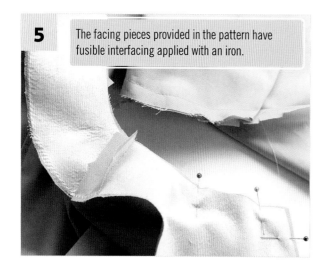

**5**

The facing pieces provided in the pattern have fusible interfacing applied with an iron.

Line up the facing by matching the center front point followed by the notches to the center back, and pin.

**6**

The collar is sandwiched between the shirt and the facing.

Continue to pin the facing along the front and neck edges. Be sure to keep the pieces smooth and flat.

**7**

Using the recommended seam allowance, begin straight stitching up the center front and pivot the corner to continue sewing around the neck opening and down the other side.

**8**

Use a point turner to get crisp, pointed corners.

Trim corners and curves using the techniques you learned earlier in the book. Grade the seam allowances for a crisp edge. Turn the fabric right side out.

**9**

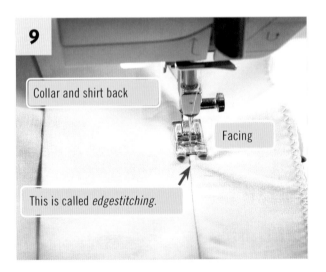

Collar and shirt back

Facing

This is called *edgestitching*.

With the seam allowance pointing down toward the facing and the shirt back pushed out of the way, straight stitch along the neck seam.

# Setting a Sleeve

Once you've created a sleeve, you'll be ready to attach it to the shirt. This is called *setting a sleeve*. The key to a comfortable sleeve is adding a bit of ease in the shoulder. Easing is similar to gathering, but doesn't create tucks or visible gathers.

Here are the basic steps for setting a sleeve; refer to your pattern instructions for specifics on the type of sleeve and attachment.

## What You Need

- Standard foot attachment
- Fabric marking tool
- Iron
- Straight pins
- Scissors
- Narrow ironing sleeve board (or rolled towel)

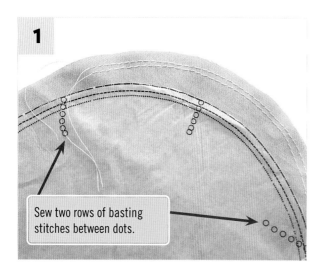

**1**

Sew two rows of basting stitches between dots.

Once the sleeve is cut, sew two rows of basting stitches between the EASE dot marks.

**2**

Sew the sleeve side seam, and press open with an iron on a sleeve board. If you don't have a sleeve board, roll up a towel tightly and slide the sleeve over it to press the seam.

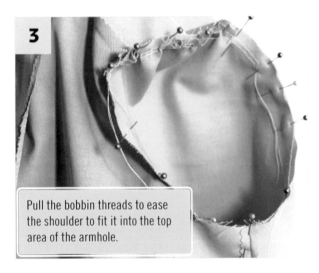

**3**

Pull the bobbin threads to ease the shoulder to fit it into the top area of the armhole.

With the sleeve right side out and the shirt inside out, begin pinning the sleeve to the armhole. Match up the notches and underarm seam.

**4**

Sew with a standard straight stitch around the entire armhole, just past the ease stitching. Be careful not to sew any tucks or folds.

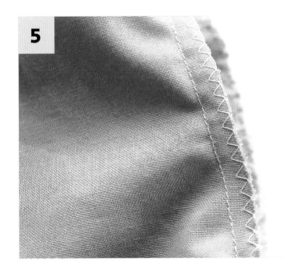

**5**

Trim the seam allowance to ¼ inch (.6 cm). Use a basic zigzag stitch around the edge of the armhole to finish the seam.

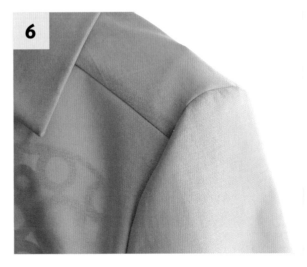

**6**

Press the seam allowance carefully; this will help to shrink up any tiny tucks or gathers. Turn the shirt right side out.

# Making a Waistband

If you can sew a straight seam, you can easily make a waistband and wow your friends with your creative talent!

Interfacing is used to give body and shape to the waistband and keep it from getting all crinkled up when the garment is worn. You can use several types of interfacing when making a waistband; for this example, I used a lightweight nonwoven fusible interfacing.

## What You Need

- Standard foot attachment
- Measuring tape
- Fabric marking tool
- Iron
- Straight pins
- Scissors
- Fusible interfacing

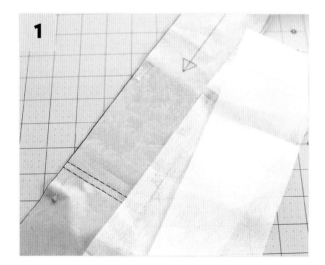

Following the pattern directions, cut your waistband out of both fabric and interfacing. Cut the interfacing slightly smaller than the fabric.

Don't overheat the glue on the interfacing or it won't stick.

Set the interfacing glue side down on the wrong side of the waistband fabric. Press quickly with an iron to heat up the glue and make it stick.

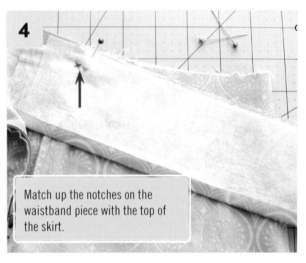

Match up the notches on the waistband piece with the top of the skirt.

Press the unnotched edge under ³⁄₈ inch (1 cm). This will make it easy to sew the final step.

Pin the waistband to the skirt. Notice the end of the waistband extends past the center back zipper about 1¹⁄₂ inches (3.75 cm) and just ⁵⁄₈ inch (1.5 cm) on the opposite side of the center-back zipper.

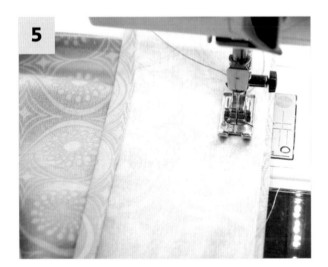

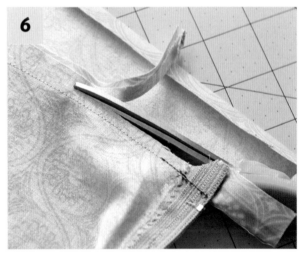

Beginning at the center back, straight stitch along the top edge at a ⁵⁄₈-inch (1.5 cm) seam allowance. Continue around to the other side of the center back opening.

Trim the seam allowance to ¹⁄₄ inch (.6 cm). Leave it untrimmed past the zipper; this will be used to create the tab that overlaps.

**7**

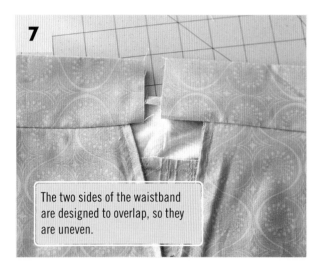

The two sides of the waistband are designed to overlap, so they are uneven.

Press the waistband up flat, keeping the top edge pressed under. The seam is pressed up toward the top.

**8**

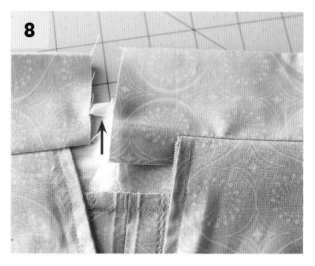

Pull the seam allowance open on the tab that extends. Fold the top edge of the waistband over toward the skirt with the right sides together, and match the edges.

**9**

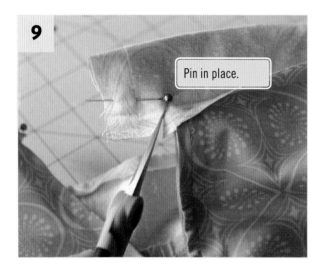

Pin in place.

Cut a tiny slit angled to the corner just before the zipper. This will allow the pressed edge to fold up while the seam allowance on the left is flat.

**10**

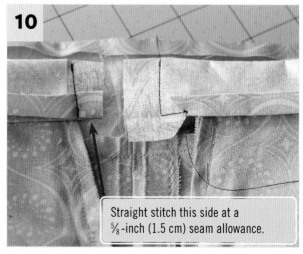

Straight stitch this side at a ⅝-inch (1.5 cm) seam allowance.

Straight stitch down from the top, pivoting at the corner, and sew a few stitches toward the pressed-up edge. Backstitch to secure.

**11**

Trim the corners and seams. Turn the two sides right side out. Following the seam from the tab, line up the pressed-under edge to just cover the seam along the inside.

**12**

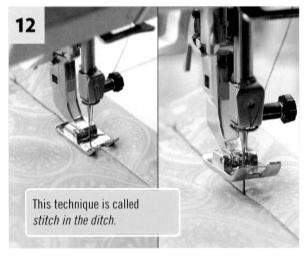

This technique is called *stitch in the ditch*.

The bottom edge of the waistband is positioned just past the seam. Straight stitch in the well of the seam. This will hide the stitching and give it a professional finish.

### Finishing Your Waistband with a Hook Closure

- Be sure to use a hook and eye closure that's designed for a skirt/waistband. It is sturdier and a bit larger than the smaller ones.
- Mark the placement of the hook on the inside of the overlap side. Mark the placement of the eye on the finished side of the opposite side of the waistband opening.
- Use the hand stitches you learned earlier in this book to secure the thread and stitch through the tiny holes along the edges. There are four holes on the eye and six holes on the hook.
- Be careful not to sew all the way through the waistband to the finished side! Simply slide the needle through just one layer of fabric.

# Curved Hems

I struggled with curved hems for a while, but once I learned this simple trick, my hems started looking great—and yours can, too!

This technique works well with a gentle curve, like on a skirt hem, and can be done on a variety of fabrics (the example is shown on cotton). Practice this a few times, and you'll never fear curved hems again!

## What You Need

- Standard foot attachment
- Seam gauge
- Fabric marking tool
- Iron
- Seam ripper
- Straight pins

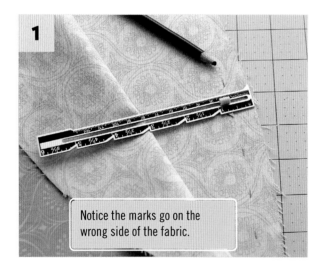

Notice the marks go on the wrong side of the fabric.

Use a seam gauge and a fabric marking tool to evenly mark a $5/8$-inch (1.5 cm) hem line around the entire curve or circle.

Sew a basting stitch along the marked line. Do not backstitch; this stitching will be taken out later.

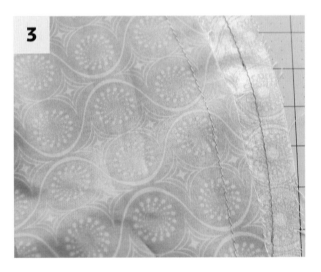

**3**

The stitching line now marks the fold line for your hem. If your fabric has excess fraying, trim it before continuing to the next step.

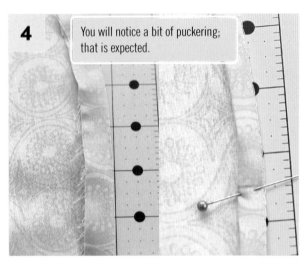

**4**

You will notice a bit of puckering; that is expected.

Press the hem up along the stitched line. Press the entire hem. Work your way around the hem a second time, this time tucking under the raw edge. Press and pin in place.

**5**

Straight stitch the hem along the top fold. Using a seam ripper, pull out the basting stitches along the bottom edge.

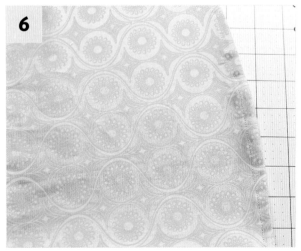

**6**

Turn the fabric right side out, and press the hem again for a finished look.

# French Seams

A French seam encloses the raw edges of the fabric on the inside of the seam. This advanced way to finish a seam is best used on sheer or lightweight fabrics.

While the technique is simple, you must pay special attention to the direction of the fabric to be sure you end up with the correct finished side.

## What You Need

- Standard foot attachment
- Scissors
- Iron
- Fabric *or* existing project

The finished side of the fabric is facing out!

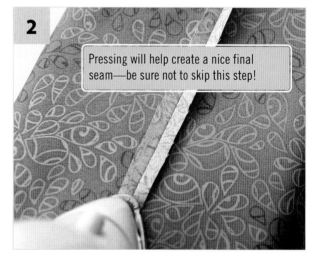

Pressing will help create a nice final seam—be sure not to skip this step!

Place two pieces of fabric with the wrong sides together. Sew a straight seam at ¼ inch (.6 cm) (this will fit into the standard ⅝-inch [1.5 cm] seam allowance).

Open up the fabric, and press the seam open flat.

**3**

If you're using a sheer fabric, be sure to cut off all the loose threads.

Being careful not to cut the body of the fabric, trim the seam allowance as close to the seam as you can (about $\frac{1}{8}$ inch [.3 cm]).

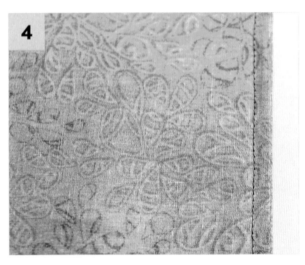

**4**

Fold the fabric back so the first seam is enclosed. The right sides of the fabric should now be facing each other.

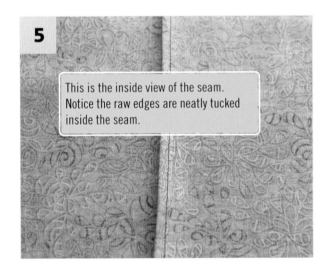

**5**

This is the inside view of the seam. Notice the raw edges are neatly tucked inside the seam.

Sew a straight seam at $\frac{1}{4}$ inch (.6 cm).

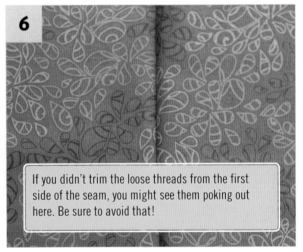

**6**

If you didn't trim the loose threads from the first side of the seam, you might see them poking out here. Be sure to avoid that!

Turn over the fabric to see the finished side of the seam. Clip any stray threads that might be poking out through the seam if necessary.

# Practice Project: Pocket Tee

If you'd like to give a plain tee some flair, try adding a cute pocket. Some contrasting fabric and a bit of trim make a statement, while the placement of the pocket down on the hip adds a bit of interest. You can do this in a variety of ways and place the pocket anywhere you like.

## What You Need

- Knowledge of straight seams, pockets, and casings
- Level of difficulty: Beginner/easy
- 9× 5-inch (23×12.75 cm) piece fabric
- 5-inch (12.75 cm) piece $1/4$-inch-wide (.6 cm) elastic
- Straight pins
- Safety pin
- 9-inch (23 cm) piece trim
- Sewing machine
- Marking tool
- Iron

**1**

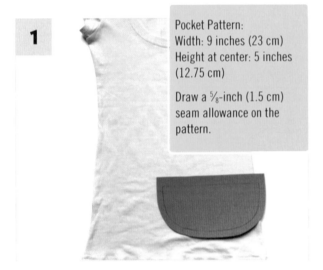

Pocket Pattern:
Width: 9 inches (23 cm)
Height at center: 5 inches (12.75 cm)

Draw a ⅝-inch (1.5 cm) seam allowance on the pattern.

Decide the pocket shape and placement, and mark the tee. Cut the pocket fabric using the template created. For the pocket here, it's simply a rectangle cut with a gentle curve at the bottom corners.

**2**

Create a casing for the elastic at the top edge of the pocket by placing the trim on the right side and straight stitching along the top edge to cover the casing seam.

**3**

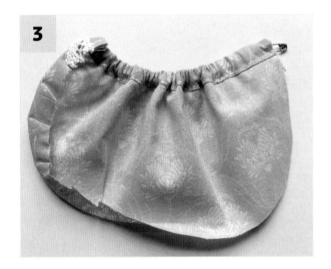

Use a safety pin to pull the elastic through the casing. Secure the safety pin to the end so the elastic doesn't pull all the way through.

**4**

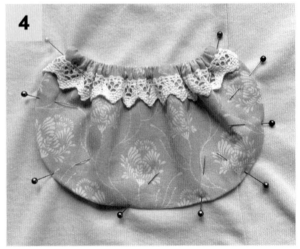

Press the raw edges under ⅝ inch (1.5 cm). Pin the pocket to the tee. Straight stitch right at the edge all the way around the sides, leaving the top of the pocket open.

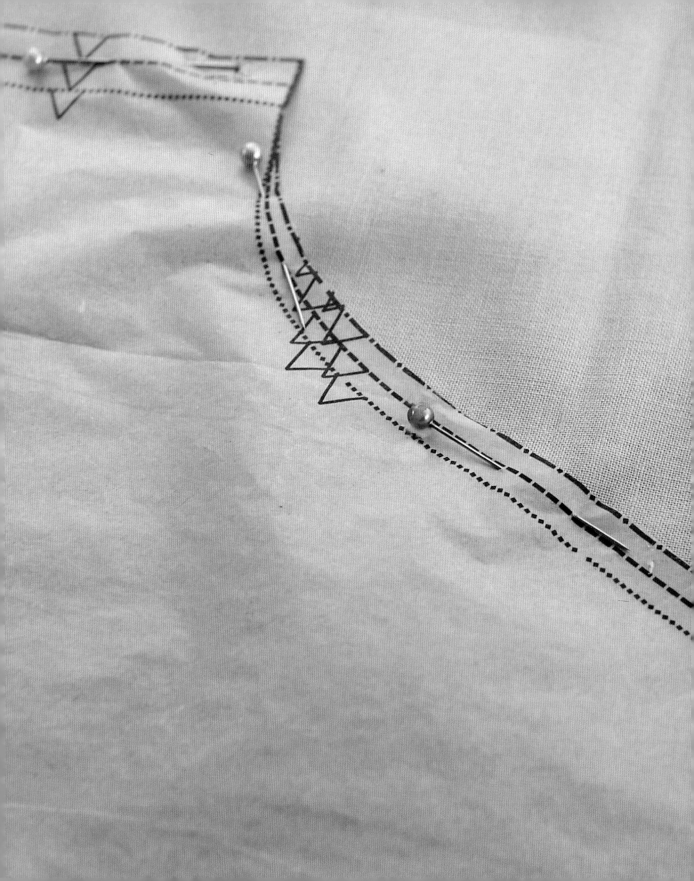

# Chapter 12

## Patterns

Reading the Envelope
Understanding the Markings
Laying Out and Cutting the Pieces

# Reading the Envelope

Many different patterns are available with envelopes of varying layouts, but one thing they all have in common is the information on them. Here, I provide an example to show you what you'll find on pattern envelopes.

Number of pattern pieces

Code number for ordering

Description of garment or item, giving details of style and different views included in pattern

List of pattern sizes in metric and imperial measurements for bust, waist, and hips in each size

Suggested fabrics suitable for garment or item as well as unsuitable fabrics

Notions required for each view

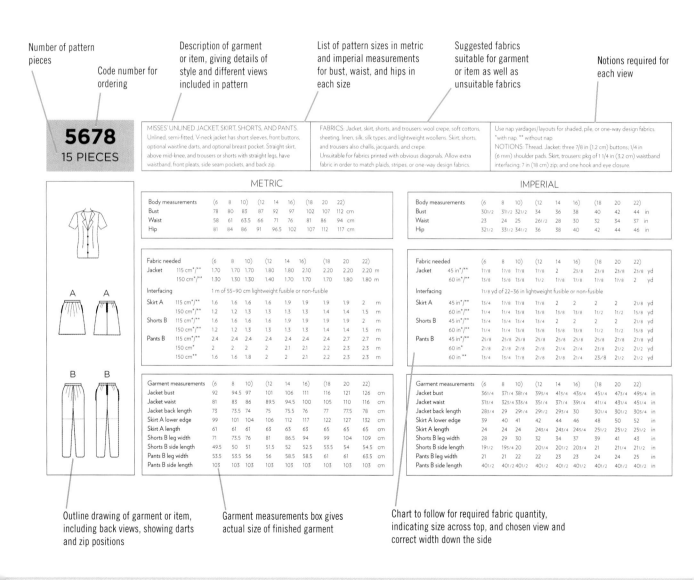

**5678**
**15 PIECES**

MISSES' UNLINED JACKET, SKIRT, SHORTS, AND PANTS. Unlined, semi-fitted, V-neck jacket has short sleeves, front buttons, optional waistline darts, and optional breast pocket. Straight skirt, above mid-knee, and trousers or shorts with straight legs, have waistband, front pleats, side seam pockets, and back zip.

FABRICS: Jacket, skirt, shorts, and trousers: wool crepe, soft cottons, sheeting, linen, silk, silk types, and lightweight woollens. Skirt, shorts, and trousers also challis, jacquards, and crepe. Unsuitable for fabrics printed with obvious diagonals. Allow extra fabric in order to match plaids, stripes, or one-way design fabrics.

Use nap yardages/layouts for shaded, pile, or one-way design fabrics. *with nap. ** without nap
NOTIONS: Thread. Jacket: three 7/8 (1.2 cm) buttons; 1/4 in (6 mm) shoulder pads. Skirt, trousers: pkg of 1 1/4 in (3.2 cm) waistband interfacing; 7 in (18 cm) zip; and one hook and eye closure.

## METRIC

| Body measurements | | (6 | 8 | 10) | (12 | 14 | 16) | (18 | 20 | 22) | |
|---|---|---|---|---|---|---|---|---|---|---|---|
| Bust | | 78 | 80 | 83 | 87 | 92 | 97 | 102 | 107 | 112 | cm |
| Waist | | 58 | 61 | 63.5 | 66 | 71 | 76 | 81 | 86 | 94 | cm |
| Hip | | 81 | 84 | 86 | 91 | 96.5 | 102 | 107 | 112 | 117 | cm |

| Fabric needed | | (6 | 8 | 10) | (12 | 14 | 16) | (18 | 20 | 22) | |
|---|---|---|---|---|---|---|---|---|---|---|---|
| Jacket | 115 cm*/** | 1.70 | 1.70 | 1.70 | 1.80 | 1.80 | 2.10 | 2.20 | 2.20 | 2.20 | m |
| | 150 cm*/** | 1.30 | 1.30 | 1.30 | 1.40 | 1.70 | 1.70 | 1.70 | 1.80 | 1.80 | m |
| Interfacing | 1 m of 55–90 cm lightweight fusible or non-fusible | | | | | | | | | | |
| Skirt A | 115 cm*/** | 1.6 | 1.6 | 1.6 | 1.6 | 1.9 | 1.9 | 1.9 | 1.9 | 2 | m |
| | 150 cm*/** | 1.2 | 1.2 | 1.3 | 1.3 | 1.3 | 1.3 | 1.4 | 1.4 | 1.5 | m |
| Shorts B | 115 cm*/** | 1.6 | 1.6 | 1.6 | 1.6 | 1.9 | 1.9 | 1.9 | 1.9 | 2 | m |
| | 150 cm*/** | 1.2 | 1.2 | 1.3 | 1.3 | 1.3 | 1.3 | 1.4 | 1.4 | 1.5 | m |
| Pants B | 115 cm*/** | 2.4 | 2.4 | 2.4 | 2.4 | 2.4 | 2.4 | 2.4 | 2.7 | 2.7 | m |
| | 150 cm* | 2 | 2 | 2 | 2 | 2.1 | 2.1 | 2.2 | 2.3 | 2.3 | m |
| | 150 cm** | 1.6 | 1.6 | 1.8 | 2 | 2 | 2.1 | 2.2 | 2.3 | 2.3 | m |

| Garment measurements | (6 | 8 | 10) | (12 | 14 | 16) | (18 | 20 | 22) | |
|---|---|---|---|---|---|---|---|---|---|---|
| Jacket bust | 92 | 94.5 | 97 | 101 | 106 | 111 | 116 | 121 | 126 | cm |
| Jacket waist | 81 | 83 | 86 | 89.5 | 94.5 | 100 | 105 | 110 | 116 | cm |
| Jacket back length | 73 | 73.5 | 74 | 75 | 75.5 | 76 | 77 | 77.5 | 78 | cm |
| Skirt A lower edge | 99 | 101 | 104 | 106 | 112 | 117 | 122 | 127 | 132 | cm |
| Skirt A length | 61 | 61 | 61 | 63 | 63 | 63 | 65 | 65 | 65 | cm |
| Shorts B leg width | 71 | 73.5 | 76 | 81 | 86.5 | 94 | 99 | 104 | 109 | cm |
| Shorts B side length | 49.5 | 50 | 51 | 51.5 | 52 | 52.5 | 53.5 | 54 | 54.5 | cm |
| Pants B leg width | 53.5 | 53.5 | 56 | 56 | 58.5 | 58.5 | 61 | 61 | 63.5 | cm |
| Pants B side length | 103 | 103 | 103 | 103 | 103 | 103 | 103 | 103 | 103 | cm |

## IMPERIAL

| Body measurements | | (6 | 8 | 10) | (12 | 14 | 16) | (18 | 20 | 22) | |
|---|---|---|---|---|---|---|---|---|---|---|---|
| Bust | | 30 1/2 | 31 1/2 | 32 1/2 | 34 | 36 | 38 | 40 | 42 | 44 | in |
| Waist | | 23 | 24 | 25 | 26 1/2 | 28 | 30 | 32 | 34 | 37 | in |
| Hip | | 32 1/2 | 33 1/2 | 34 1/2 | 36 | 38 | 40 | 42 | 44 | 46 | in |

| Fabric needed | | (6 | 8 | 10) | (12 | 14 | 16) | (18 | 20 | 22) | |
|---|---|---|---|---|---|---|---|---|---|---|---|
| Jacket | 45 in*/** | 1 7/8 | 1 7/8 | 1 7/8 | 1 7/8 | 2 | 2 3/8 | 2 3/8 | 2 3/8 | 2 5/8 | yd |
| | 60 in*/** | 1 3/8 | 1 3/8 | 1 3/8 | 1 1/2 | 1 7/8 | 1 7/8 | 1 7/8 | 1 7/8 | 2 | yd |
| Interfacing | 1 1/8 yd of 22–36 in lightweight fusible or non-fusible | | | | | | | | | | |
| Skirt A | 45 in*/** | 1 3/4 | 1 7/8 | 1 7/8 | 1 7/8 | 2 | 2 | 2 | 2 | 2 1/8 | yd |
| | 60 in*/** | 1 1/4 | 1 1/4 | 1 3/8 | 1 3/8 | 1 3/8 | 1 3/8 | 1 1/2 | 1 1/2 | 1 5/8 | yd |
| Shorts B | 45 in*/** | 1 3/4 | 1 3/4 | 1 3/4 | 1 3/4 | 2 | 2 | 2 | 2 | 2 1/8 | yd |
| | 60 in*/** | 1 1/4 | 1 1/4 | 1 3/8 | 1 3/8 | 1 3/8 | 1 3/8 | 1 1/2 | 1 1/2 | 1 5/8 | yd |
| Pants B | 45 in*/** | 2 5/8 | 2 5/8 | 2 5/8 | 2 5/8 | 2 5/8 | 2 5/8 | 2 5/8 | 2 7/8 | 2 7/8 | yd |
| | 60 in* | 2 1/8 | 2 1/8 | 2 1/8 | 2 1/8 | 2 1/4 | 2 1/4 | 2 3/8 | 2 1/2 | 2 1/2 | yd |
| | 60 in ** | 1 3/4 | 1 3/4 | 1 7/8 | 2 1/8 | 2 1/8 | 2 1/4 | 2 3/8 | 2 1/2 | 2 1/2 | yd |

| Garment measurements | (6 | 8 | 10) | (12 | 14 | 16) | (18 | 20 | 22) | |
|---|---|---|---|---|---|---|---|---|---|---|
| Jacket bust | 36 1/4 | 37 1/4 | 38 1/4 | 39 3/4 | 41 3/4 | 43 3/4 | 45 1/4 | 47 3/4 | 49 3/4 | in |
| Jacket waist | 31 1/2 | 32 3/4 | 33 3/4 | 35 1/4 | 37 1/4 | 39 1/4 | 41 1/4 | 43 1/4 | 45 1/4 | in |
| Jacket back length | 28 3/4 | 29 | 29 1/4 | 29 1/2 | 29 3/4 | 30 | 30 1/4 | 30 1/2 | 30 3/4 | in |
| Skirt A lower edge | 39 | 40 | 41 | 42 | 44 | 46 | 48 | 50 | 52 | in |
| Skirt A length | 24 | 24 | 24 | 24 3/4 | 24 3/4 | 24 3/4 | 25 1/2 | 25 1/2 | 25 1/2 | in |
| Shorts B leg width | 28 | 29 | 30 | 32 | 34 | 37 | 39 | 41 | 43 | in |
| Shorts B side length | 19 1/2 | 19 3/4 | 20 | 20 1/4 | 20 1/2 | 20 3/4 | 21 | 21 1/4 | 21 1/2 | in |
| Pants B leg width | 21 | 21 | 22 | 22 | 23 | 23 | 24 | 24 | 25 | in |
| Pants B side length | 40 1/2 | 40 1/2 | 40 1/2 | 40 1/2 | 40 1/2 | 40 1/2 | 40 1/2 | 40 1/2 | 40 1/2 | in |

Outline drawing of garment or item, including back views, showing darts and zip positions

Garment measurements box gives actual size of finished garment

Chart to follow for required fabric quantity, indicating size across top, and chosen view and correct width down the side

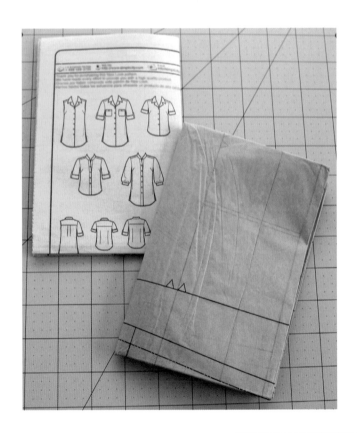

In a pattern envelope, you'll find printed instructions and pattern pieces printed on tissue paper. The instruction sheet shows the variations that can be made; each variation is labeled with a letter and corresponds to specific pattern pieces.

You will also find a cutting layout printed for each style variation. Each pattern piece will have specific markings on the pieces and images to show the right and wrong sides of the fabric.

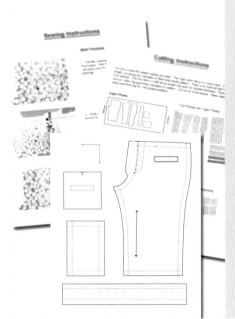

### The Exciting World of E-Patterns

E-patterns are PDFs of patterns sold online. You simply pay for the pattern, download it, and print it out on your own printer.

E-patterns usually have full-color, step-by-step pictures to walk you through your sewing project, and each picture is lined up with the text for easy readability.

The pattern pieces print out on standard, 8½ x 11-inch (21 x 28 cm) paper. Some e-patterns print out a full piece on one page. For example, a doll clothes pattern has small-enough pieces to fit all on one page.

Larger pieces, like children- and adult-size clothing patterns, are printed out and taped together to create the full-size piece.

This new style of pattern is a popular trend—just search online to see what's available!

# Understanding the Markings

To some, patterns may seem like reading Greek. However, once you become familiar with the markings, you should have no problem following the pattern instructions and successfully making something new.

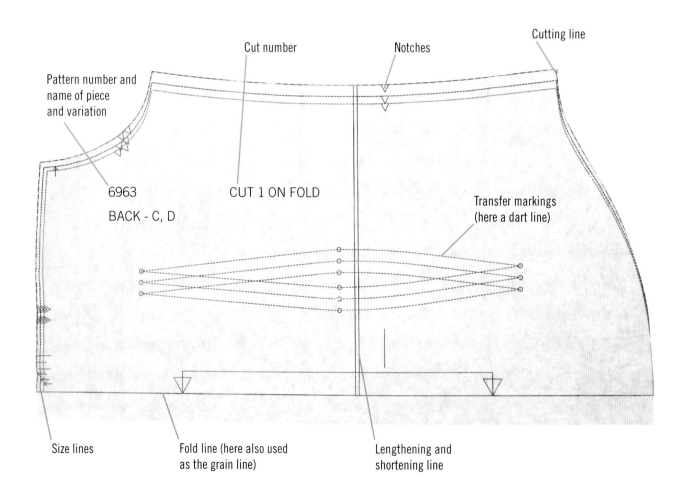

Cutting line

Cut number

Notches

Pattern number and name of piece and variation

6963
BACK - C, D

CUT 1 ON FOLD

Transfer markings (here a dart line)

Size lines

Fold line (here also used as the grain line)

Lengthening and shortening line

## Important things to notice:

- The **grain line** is a line with an arrow at each end. Line up the piece so the grain is the same as the fabric. Most grain line arrows go straight up and down, while some are on the diagonal.

- Place the **fold line** on the folded edge of the fabric; don't cut along this side.

- You can **lengthen** a pattern by cutting it apart on the designated lines and adding the desired amount in between the two pieces. Simply tape them together to create a longer piece. Be sure to add the same amount to any other piece—for example, the front and back of a shirt should both be lengthened equal amounts.

- Notice any **transfer markings** on the pattern, such as button or buttonhole placement, dart lines, or pocket guides. These markings will need to be drawn on the actual fabric piece.

- **Notches** are used to match up certain sections of two different pieces. Cut them out into the seam allowance, away from the pattern piece.

- Pay attention to the **"cut" number**. Is it cut 1 on fold, cut 1, or cut 2? This is very important. Be sure to notice this when deciding the best layout of all the pieces on your fabric. If your piece is cut 1, you will not need to have the fabric folded with two layers when cutting it out.

- The **cutting line** is the thin black line around the outside edge of the piece. Cut just outside it through the fabric.

- Multi-size patterns are available to cut at different sizes. Each **size line** is dashed and dotted in a different pattern. Pay special attention to this when cutting out your desired size.

Patterns include a set of universal symbols and markings. Here is what you'll find:

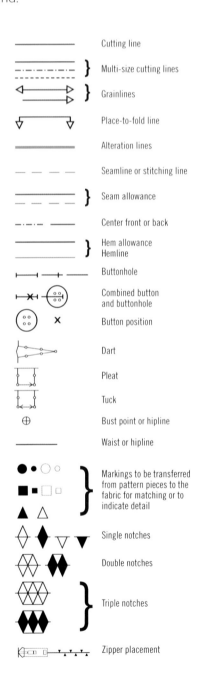

| | |
|---|---|
| | Cutting line |
| | Multi-size cutting lines |
| | Grainlines |
| | Place-to-fold line |
| | Alteration lines |
| | Seamline or stitching line |
| | Seam allowance |
| | Center front or back |
| | Hem allowance / Hemline |
| | Buttonhole |
| | Combined button and buttonhole |
| | Button position |
| | Dart |
| | Pleat |
| | Tuck |
| | Bust point or hipline |
| | Waist or hipline |
| | Markings to be transferred from pattern pieces to the fabric for matching or to indicate detail |
| | Single notches |
| | Double notches |
| | Triple notches |
| | Zipper placement |

# Laying Out and Cutting
## the Pieces

When laying out and cutting the pieces for your project, pay attention to the grain line arrows on each pattern piece and identify the grain of the fabric—lining these two up will give you the finished results you're looking for. Also, follow the layout diagram so you're sure you can fit all the pieces on the recommended amount of fabric.

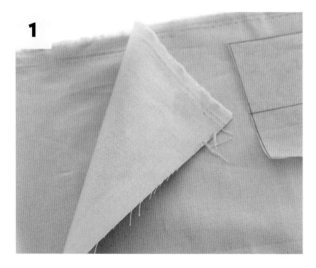

**1**

Fold your fabric in half lengthwise, with the right sides together. Your pattern may have special diagrams that show a different folding method, so check it for specifics.

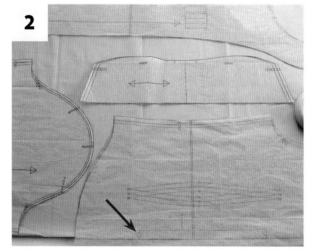

**2**

Some pieces may lay with the writing face down to fit better on the fabric. Leave enough space between pieces to comfortably cut them out.

**3**

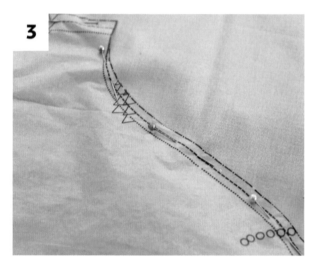

Starting at the top side, poke a pin down through all layers and then back up to the top. Pin around the edges of the pattern pieces, keeping a few inches of space in between.

**4**

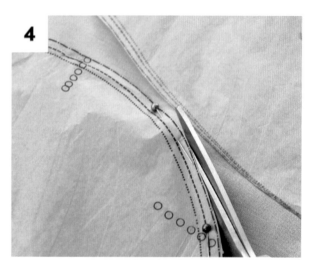

Lift the fabric just enough to slide the scissors underneath—the bottom blade should slide along the table or mat. Cut just outside the pattern piece, through both layers of fabric. Place your other hand flat on the fabric to hold it in place.

**5**

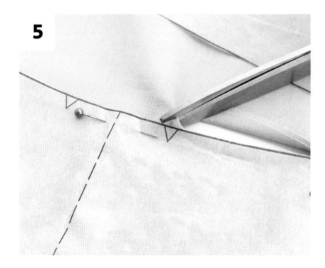

Pay attention to the marks on the pattern piece. When you come across a notch marking, be sure to cut it outward, forming a small triangle on the outside edge of the seam allowance.

**6**

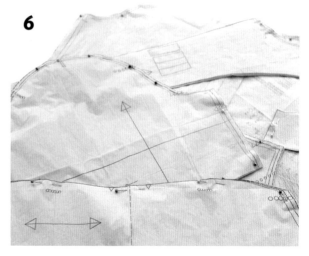

Once you have all of the pieces cut out, see if there are any special markings that should be transferred onto the fabric, such as dart lines or ease stitching points.

# Part 4
# A Gallery of Projects

Basic Projects
Easy Projects
Intermediate Projects

# Basic Project 1:
# Peppermint Coasters

Whether you're planning a casual get-together or a festive holiday party, these cute coasters will set the theme!

Reminiscent of peppermint Christmas candies, these coasters made with felt are the perfect project for you to practice your hand-sewing stitches. This project requires very little experience and doesn't use a sewing machine, which is perfect for a beginner.

## What You Need

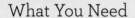

- Knowledge of hand sewing a running stitch
- 2 colored felt squares
- 1 white felt square
- 6×4-inch (15×10 cm) piece fusible web, such as Wonder Under
- Embroidery thread in two colors that match the felt colors
- Hand-sewing needle with large eye
- Scissors
- Straight pins
- Iron
- Traced pattern pieces from this book

**1**

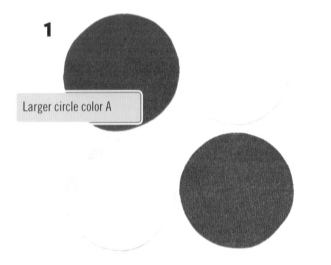

Larger circle color A

Using the pattern pieces provided, cut one larger circle from color A and one of each color from the smaller circle pattern. Cut two pieces of the fusible web.

**2**

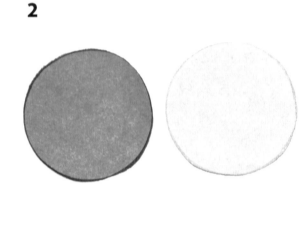

Place the fusible web on the backside of the felt, paper side facing up. Iron for just a few seconds to fuse it to the felt.

**3**

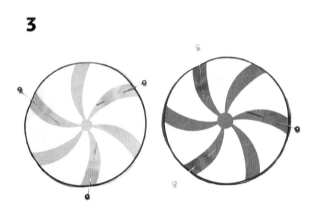

Place the color B pattern on top of the color B felt circle. Pin inside the colored areas; the white sections will be removed. Repeat for color A.

**4**

Cut out the swirl pattern, being careful as you get close to the center of the circle. Repeat for color A.

**5**

The paper backing is still applied to the backside of each swirl color that you've now cut out.

**6**

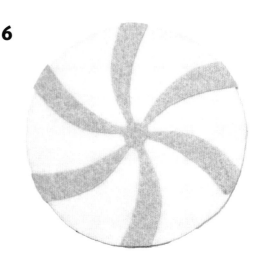

Peel off the paper backing from swirl B and place it on top of the white felt circle. Press with an iron to fuse the two fabrics together.

**7**

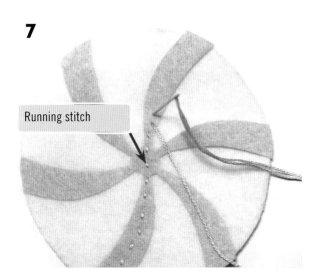

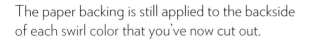

Running stitch

Cut a 2-foot (61 cm) length of embroidery thread, and separate in half. Thread your needle with the three strands. Starting from under the white side, sew a running stitch down the center of each swirl.

**8**

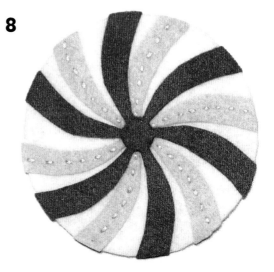

Place the color A swirl on top of the color B swirl and rotate so the swirls fit in the white spaces between the color B swirls. Press to fuse the color A swirl.

**9**

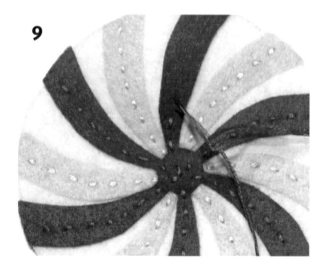

Use a running stitch and sew down the center of each color A swirl, keeping the stitches evenly spaced. Secure the knots on the backside.

**10**

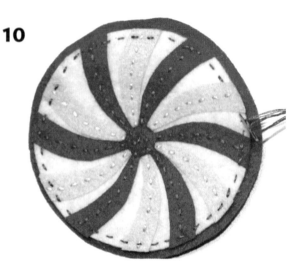

Place the white circle on top of the large color A circle. Using a running stitch, sew around the outside edge of the white circle to complete.

Use below pattern for swirl placement

The pattern pieces should be traced onto paper and cut out.

Coaster Base: Cut 1 of felt color A

Swirl Pattern: Cut 1 of felt color A

Swirl pattern: Cut 1 of felt color B

Circle pattern: Cut 1 of felt color white, and 2 of Wonder Under

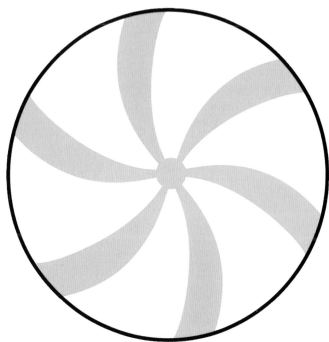

# Basic Project 2: Elastic-Waist Skirt

Did you know you can make a skirt without using a pattern? You can—and it's really easy, too! The skirt featured here is made from lightweight, woven cotton fabric cut into a long rectangle, has an elastic casing at the waist, and is accented with a tiny trim along the hemline. This is the simplest type of skirt to make. Why not make several and have a new skirt for every day of the week?

## What You Need

- Knowledge of straight seams, elastic casing, and attaching trim

- 44-inch-wide × 20-inch-tall (111.75 × 51 cm) cotton fabric (this fits a 28-inch [71 cm] waist)

- To customize the size: width = 9 inches (23 cm) + hip measurement; length = 3 inches (7.5 cm) + desired length (for example, from waist to knee)

- 45-inch-long (114.25 cm) trim

- 2-inch-wide (5 cm) elastic 29 inches (74 cm) in length

- Straight and safety pins

- Sewing machine

- Measuring tape

- Scissors

- Iron

- Seam gauge

**1**

Cut out the skirt fabric to the specified measurements. Measure and cut the elastic and the trim piece.

**2**

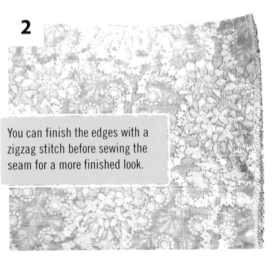

You can finish the edges with a zigzag stitch before sewing the seam for a more finished look.

With the right sides together, fold the skirt fabric in half, matching up the two short sides. Sew a straight seam with a ⅝-inch (1.5 cm) seam allowance.

**3**

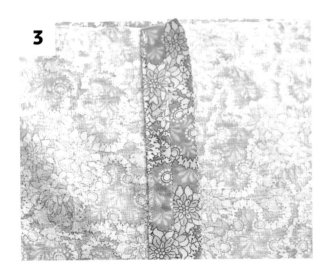

Lay the skirt flat, and press the seam open.

**4**

Create a narrow hem along the bottom edge of the skirt by folding twice at ¼ inch (.6 cm). Press and pin to hold it in place.

**5**

Position the trim so it hangs past the edge of the fabric.

Turn the skirt to the right side, and carefully pin the trim to the pinned hemline. Straight stitch to secure the trim and create the hem.

**6**

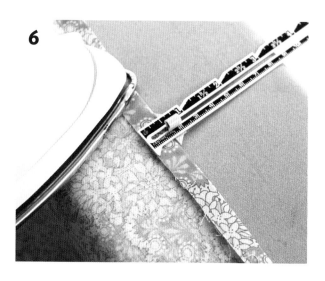

Create an elastic casing by first pressing the top edge of the skirt under ½ inch (1.25 cm). Do this around the entire top edge.

**7**

The seam gauge will help you create a nice, consistent casing.

Measure 2 ¼ inches (5.75 cm), and fold the top edge over again all the way around the skirt to create the casing for the elastic.

**8**

Straight stitch along the bottom folded edge, leaving a 3-inch (7.5 cm) opening to feed in the elastic.

**9**

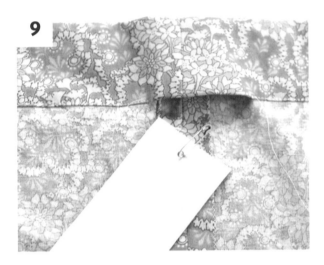

Secure a safety pin in the end of the elastic. Feed it into the casing, and pull it all the way through so it comes out the other side. Be sure to keep the other end out of the casing.

**10**

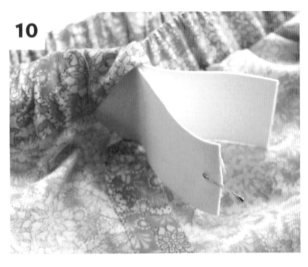

Scrunch up the fabric over the elastic and pull both ends out so you have enough space to fit them under your sewing machine foot.

**11**

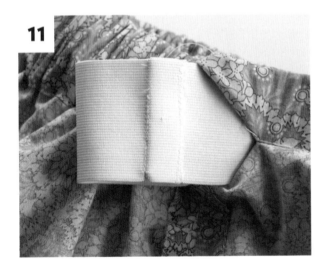

Remove the safety pin, and sew the two ends together. Zigzag stitch down the seam allowance so it lies flat on the elastic.

**12**

Slide the elastic into the casing and stitch the opening closed, by hand or by machine. The skirt is now ready to wear!

# Basic Project 3:
## Mannequin Scissor Holder

Tiny, 4-inch (10 cm) embroidery scissors are a sewing essential, so why not make a nice holder for them? This mannequin-inspired scissor holder is a fun accessory and a great way to keep those super-pointy scissors visible and protected. It's a perfect project to use up scraps of fabric and trim.

## What You Need

- Knowledge of straight and zigzag seams, cutting out a pattern, attaching trims, and layering fabrics
- 8 × 8-inch (20.25×20.25 cm) piece fabric A
- 8 × 4-inch (20.25×10 cm) piece fabric B
- 8×4-inch (20.25×10 cm) piece heavy-weight fusible interfacing
- 8×4-inch (20.25×10 cm) piece quilt batting
- Assorted trim pieces
- Scissors
- Straight pins
- Iron
- Traced pattern pieces from this book

**1**

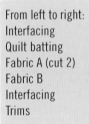

From left to right:
Interfacing
Quilt batting
Fabric A (cut 2)
Fabric B
Interfacing
Trims

Cut out all pieces using the provided pattern pieces.

**2**

Place the interfacing on the wrong side of the mannequin piece (fabric A), being sure to place fusible side down and pressing with a hot iron.

**3**

The trim should overlap ½ inch (1.25 cm).

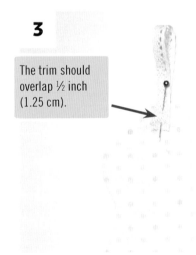

Cut a 4¹/₂-inch (11.5 cm) piece of trim for the hanger loop. Fold the trim in half and pin it to the wrong side of the mannequin, making sure to center it at the top. Baste stitch in place.

**4**

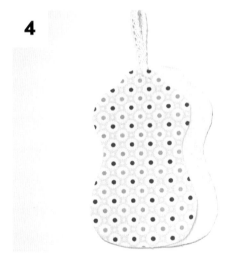

Lay down the second mannequin piece, wrong side up. Place the quilt batting on top and the interfaced mannequin piece on top of that, right side up. Line up all the edges.

**5**

Pin through all three layers. Using ¹⁄₄-inch (.6 cm) seam allowances, stitch around the outside edge, being sure to keep all the edges lined up and the fabric flat.

**6**

The interfacing only covers half of the piece.

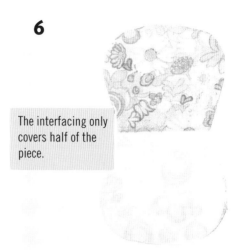

Place the pocket interfacing, fusible side own, onto the wrong side of the pocket. Press with a hot iron to fuse.

**7**

Fold the pocket piece in half, wrong sides together, to form the pocket. Sew the desired trim pieces to the topside of the pocket. Baste stitch around the pocket edges.

**8**

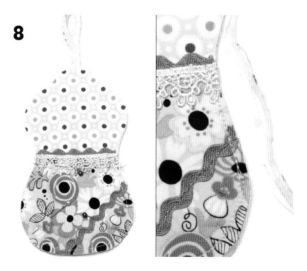

Place the pocket, right side up, on the right side of the mannequin piece. Pin in place, and baste stitch the pocket to the mannequin. Trim the seam to ¹⁄₈ inch (.3 cm), and sew a satin stitch around the outside edge.

The pattern pieces should be traced onto tissue paper.

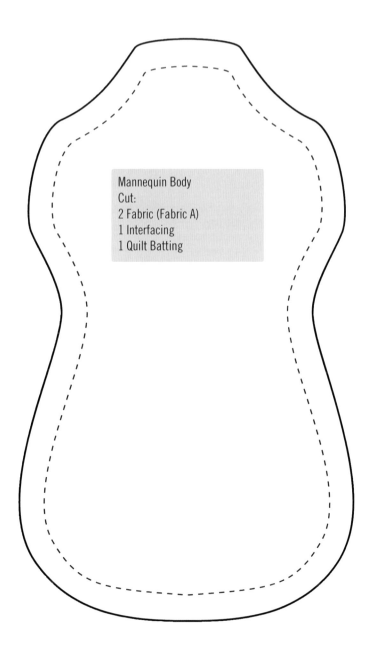

Mannequin Body
Cut:
2 Fabric (Fabric A)
1 Interfacing
1 Quilt Batting

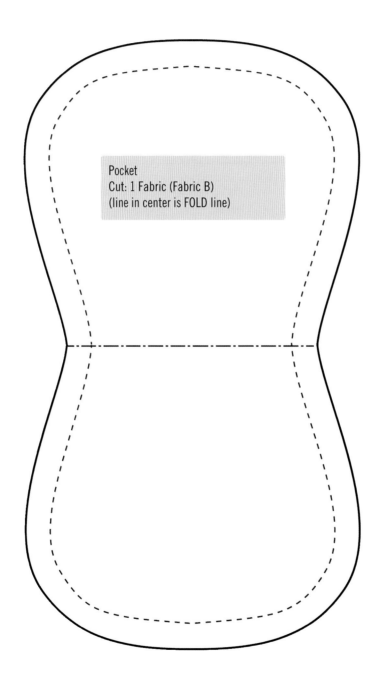

Pocket
Cut: 1 Fabric (Fabric B)
(line in center is FOLD line)

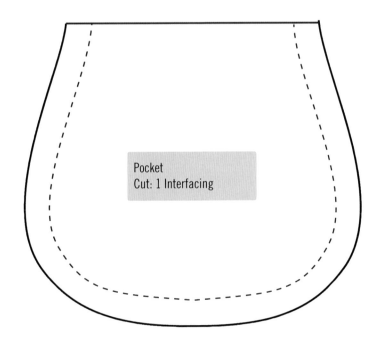

Pocket
Cut: 1 Interfacing

# Basic Project 4: Felt Coffee Cozy

A felt coffee cozy is a perfect first sewing project. It has just two pieces to cut out, uses felt fabric that doesn't need to be hemmed, and has very few steps to follow to complete it. Whether you're drinking coffee, tea, or a yummy cup of hot cocoa, your hands will thank you for this cozy.

## What You Need

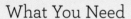

- Knowledge of straight seams and zigzag stitching
- Felt fabric in one color
- Fleece fabric in one color (you can also use felt for the top layer)
- Scissors
- Pinking shears
- Sewing machine
- Hand-sewing needle
- Traced, cut-out pattern piece from this book

**1**

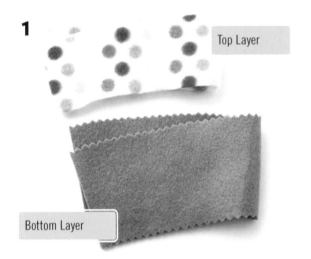

Top Layer

Bottom Layer

Cut out the fabrics using the provided pattern pieces. Cut the top and bottom edges of the bottom layer of felt with pinking shears for a decorative look.

**2**

Place the print top layer on top of the blue bottom layer, centering it so there's an equal distance at the top and bottom edges.

**3**

Sew a zigzag stitch along the top edge of the fleece, being sure to keep the fabric evenly spaced from the edge.

**4**

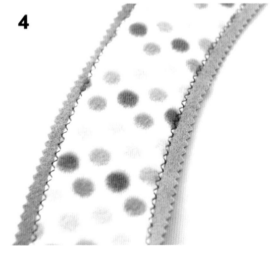

Stitch a zigzag stitch on both the top and bottom edges. The stitch should cover the raw edge.

**5**

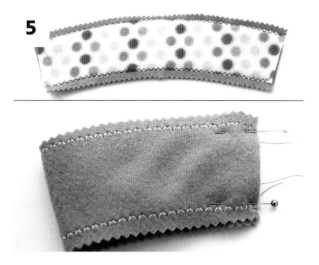

With the right sides together, fold the piece in half and line up the center back seam. Pin and straight stitch at a ¼-inch (.6 cm) seam allowance.

**6**

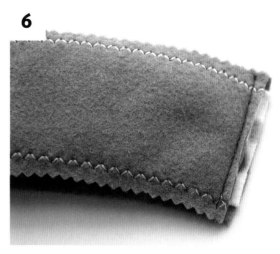

Grade the seam allowance by clipping one side of the seam close to the stitching.

**7**

Fold the seam allowance over to one side. Thread a hand-sewing needle, and stitch the edge down flat to reduce the bulk.

**8**

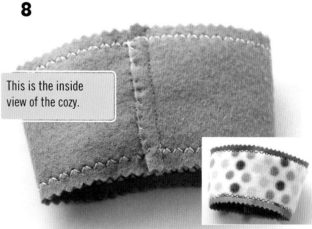

This is the inside view of the cozy.

Once the seam is stitched, secure the end and clip the threads. Turn the coffee cozy right side out, slide it onto your coffee cup, and start sipping your drink!

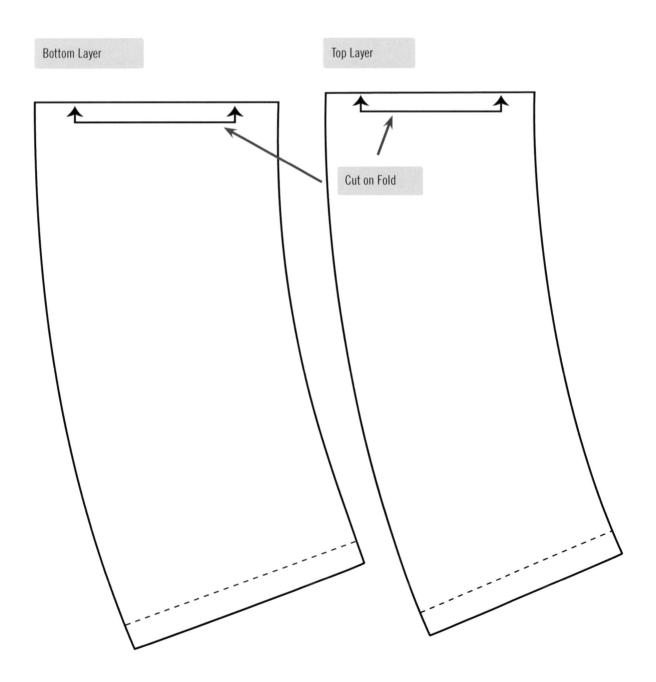

Bottom Layer

Top Layer

Cut on Fold

# Easy Project 1:
## Sewing Machine Cover

Keeping your sewing machine covered is a great way to extend the life of your machine. Most models come with a plain white cover that's just so blah! However, you can use it as a guide to create a fun and more interesting fabric cover. The cover featured here has a functional side pocket and is reversible, too. It's a great way to brighten up your sewing space!

### What You Need

- Knowledge of straight seams and sewing corners
- 27 x 45-inch (68.5 x 114.25 cm) piece *or* several smaller 7 x 8-inch (17.75 x 20.25 cm) pieces cotton fabric in coordinating colors
- Straight pins
- Measuring tape
- Scissors
- Sewing machine
- Iron

## Cover Pieces to Measure and Cut

- **Front and Back:** 4 pieces, each 17×11 3/4 inches (43×30 cm)

- **Side and Top:** 2 pieces, each 6 3/4×37 inches (17×94 cm)

- **Pocket:** 2 pieces, each 6 3/4×8 inches (17×20.25 cm)

Note: This cover fits most standard sewing machines. To customize the size to your specific machine, you can measure the manufacturer's cover and make adjustments.

**1**

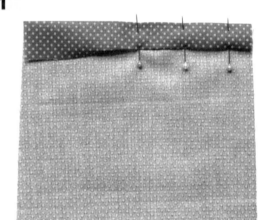

Press and fold under the top edge of the pocket to create a 3/4-inch (2 cm) hem. Pin and straight stitch along the bottom folded edge.

**2**

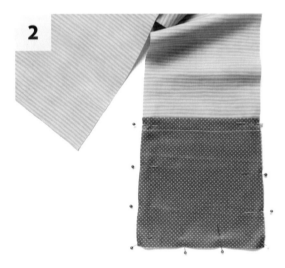

Place the pocket right side up on the bottom edge of the side piece. Pin and stitch around the sides and bottom edge. Remove the pins.

**3**

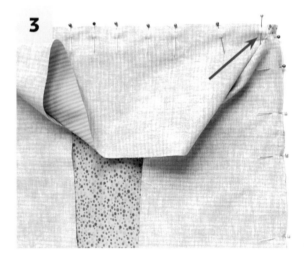

With the right sides together, pin the side piece to the back piece, lining up the edges. Clip a small slit into the seam allowance, where the side will turn the corner.

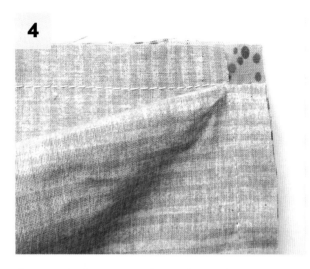

**4**

Start at the bottom and straight stitch up to the corner. Pivot, and continue sewing across the top and down the other side.

**5**

With the right sides together, pin the front piece to the other long side of the side piece. Repeat the sewing instructions in step 5.

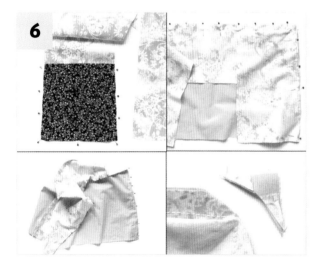

**6**

Repeat steps 2 through 6 for the inside lining pieces.

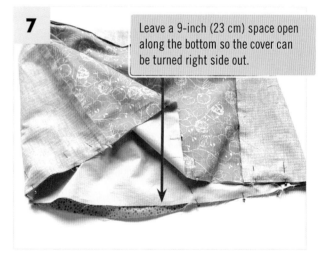

**7**

Leave a 9-inch (23 cm) space open along the bottom so the cover can be turned right side out.

With the right sides together, slide the lining inside the outside piece. Line up the front and back pieces and all of the seams. Pin around the bottom edge.

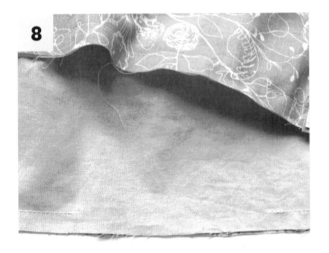

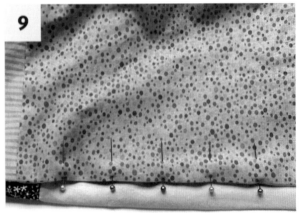

Straight stitch around the bottom edge with a ⅝-inch (1.5 cm) seam allowance. Backstitch at the beginning and end to secure. Turn the cover right side out through the opening.

Press the bottom edge flat, and turn the raw edge of the opening under ⅝ inch (1.5 cm). Fold the open section in toward the inside to line up with the seam, and pin.

**10**

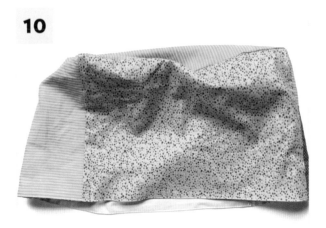

Topstitch around the entire bottom edge. Press the cover to remove any wrinkles. Slide the cover over your machine, step back, and admire your handiwork!

# Easy Project 2:
# Pincushion

Making a pincushion is a great beginning sewing project and a unique way to spruce up your sewing workspace. Pick several different fabrics that coordinate well together, and you're on your way to creating a pretty little pincushion!

## What You Need

- Small scraps cotton fabric in two colors
- 11 $\frac{1}{2}$ x 2-inch (29.25 x 5 cm) piece cotton fabric
- 50 inches (127 cm) thin ribbon or yarn
- Hand-sewing needle
- Scissors
- Straight pins
- Iron
- Stuffing or batting
- Traced pattern piece from this book

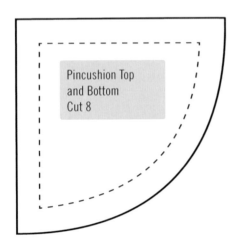

Pincushion Top
and Bottom
Cut 8

Trace the pattern pieces onto paper. Cut out the eight pieces for the pincushion, using the pattern.

**1**

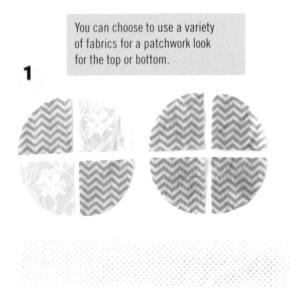

Separate into two sets of four pieces for the top and bottom.

**2**

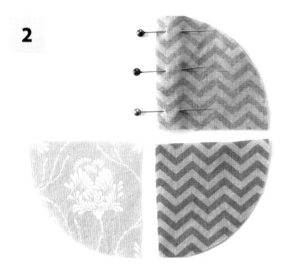

Lay out the four top pieces and with the right sides together, line up the center seam. Pin, and straight stitch.

**3**

Open up the seam and press it flat. Repeat for the bottom half of the circle.

**4**

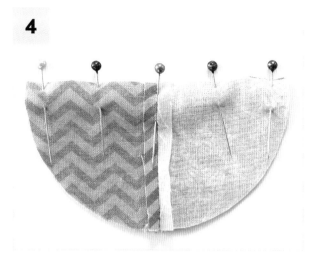

With the right sides together, line up the two halves of the circle and pin the center seam. Stitch, and press open. Repeat for the bottom circle.

**5**

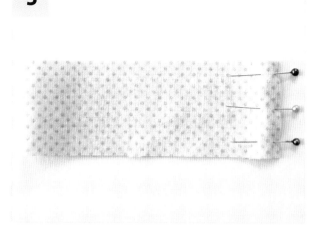

With the right sides together, fold the side piece in half, matching up the short ends. Pin, and straight stitch.

**6**

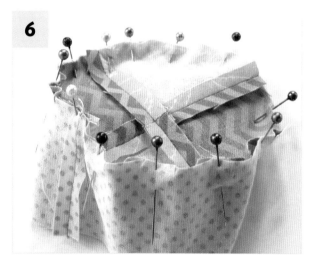

With the right sides together, pin the top circle to the side piece. Carefully straight stitch with a ¼-inch (.6 cm) seam allowance around the entire circle.

**7**

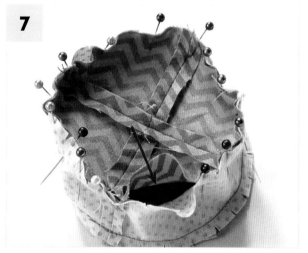

With the right sides together, pin the bottom circle into the other side. Leave a small opening to turn the piece right side out, and straight stitch.

**8**

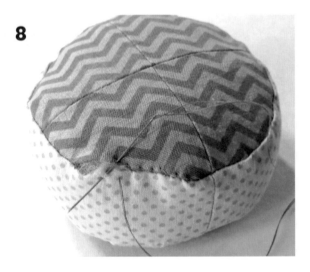

Turn the pincushion right side out, and stuff firmly with the batting. Hand sew the opening closed, being sure to secure both ends of the stitching.

**9**

Place the center of the long piece of ribbon on the center top of the pincushion. Pin to hold it in place.

**10**

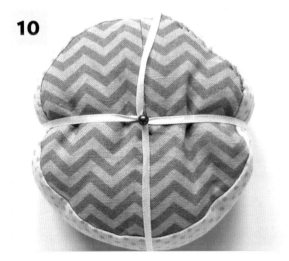

Wrap the ribbon around the bottom and crisscross to wrap back up to the top, following the seam lines. Place a pin to hold it at the center.

**11**

Continue to wrap the pincushion until it's divided into eight sections. Wrap back up to the top, and tie the ribbon in a knot or a bow. Sew through the top and bottom at the center to secure the ribbon.

# Easy Project 3:
# Tissue Pack Cover

I'm sure we all agree tissues are great to have on hand, but they look a bit boring wrapped in clear plastic. Why not dress them up with a festive fabric cover?

These covers are designed to fit the standard-size pocket packs of tissues and are made using small pieces of cotton fabric. The pieces are designed so that you can use a contrasting fabric for half of the top or just one fabric for the whole thing—the choice is up to you!

## What You Need

- Knowledge of straight seams and zigzag stitching
- 18 x 22-inch (45.75 x 56 cm) piece cotton fabric in one color (a fat quarter works great)
- Small scrap piece cotton fabric in one color (for contrast)
- 5×5-inch (12.75×12.75 cm) piece fusible non-woven interfacing
- Iron
- Straight pins
- Ruler or measuring tape
- Pinking shears
- Scissors

## Tissue Pack Cover Pieces to Measure and Cut

- **Top:** 2 pieces, each 6×2 $\frac{1}{2}$ inches (15.25×6.25 cm)

- **Bottom:** 2 pieces, each 6×5 inches (15.25×12.75 cm)

- **Interfacing:** 1 piece, 5×1 $\frac{1}{4}$ inches (12.75×3.25 cm); 1 piece, 5×3 $\frac{3}{4}$ inches (12.75×9.5 cm)

Note: You can cut the top and bottom edges of the bottom layer with pinking shears for a decorative look.

**1**

Space around the edge of the interfacing is the $\frac{5}{8}$-inch (1.5 cm) seam allowance.

Lay one of each top layer and base layer piece wrong side up. Place the interfacing on each piece, centered, with the textured fusible side down. Press to bond the interfacing to the fabric.

**2**

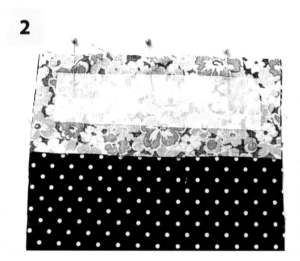

With the right sides together, place the top layer on the base layer and line up the side seam. Pin and stitch. Repeat with the other top and base pieces.

**3**

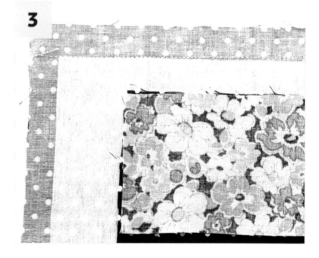

The $\frac{5}{8}$-inch (1.5 cm) seam allowance should line up just to the inside of the interfacing on the top piece. The other pieces are stitched but don't have interfacing.

**4**

Trim the seam and press the seam open flat on both pieces.

**5**

Place the two pieces on top of each other with the right sides together. Pin along the top and bottom edges. Line up the seam where the two fabrics meet.

**6**

Straight stitch along both the top and bottom edges, removing the pins as you sew.

**7**

Turn the tissue cover right side out. Press so the edges are crisp and straight.

**8**

Fold the finished ends in so they meet in the middle. Set a tissue pack in to check the fit, and pin the sides.

**9**

Remove the tissue pack, and sew a straight seam down each side. Overlap the edges about ¼ inch (.6 cm) when sewing. Trim the seam, and finish with a zigzag stitch on both sides.

**10**

Turn the cover right side out, and push the corners out to a point. Take the tissues out of the plastic wrapper, and place them inside the fabric holder.

# Easy Project 4:
# Reusable Snack Bag

Laminated cotton fabric has a glossy sheen and a protective coating on the right side of the fabric. It's easy to sew with and can be wiped off with water, so it's great to use for making reusable snack bags. This is perfect for parents on the go—just pop in some fruit or crackers and toss it in your bag for later. And because you can reuse it again and again, this bag is not only fun, it's environmentally friendly!

## What You Need

- Knowledge of straight seams, sewing corners, and attaching Velcro

- 9 x 45-inch (23 x 114.25 cm) *or* 18 × 22-inch (45.75 × 56 cm) piece laminated cotton fabric

- $1/2$-inch-wide (1.25 cm) Velcro

- Measuring tape

- Scissors

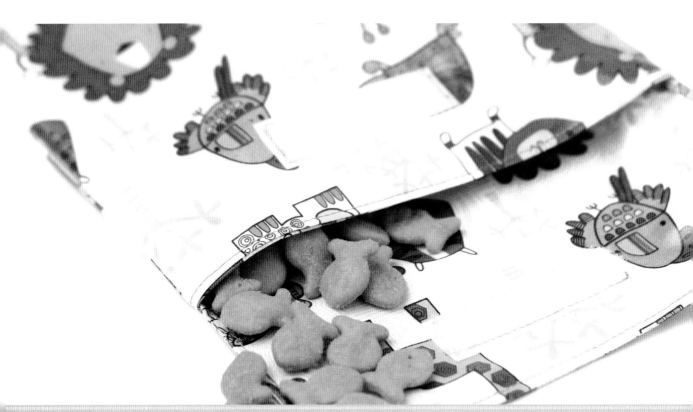

## Bag Pieces to Measure and Cut

- **Front and Back:** 2 pieces, each 8×18 inches (20.25×45.75 cm)

- **Velcro:** 1 piece (both sides), 3 inches (7.5 cm)

**1**

The shiny side is the right side.

With the right sides together, fold up the bottom edge of the rectangle, leaving 3 ½ inches (8.25 cm) of space at the top. Straight stitch with ½-inch (1.25 cm) seam allowances.

**2**

Repeat for the other rectangle. You should have two pieces that look the same.

**3**

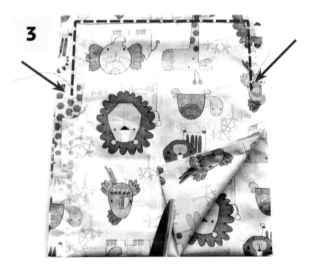

Place the two bags on top of each other, with the right sides of the top flap facing each other. Straight stitch just the top flap, and backstitch to secure.

**4**

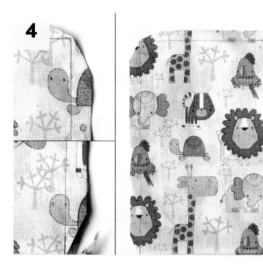

Trim the seam allowances at the corners of the flap and both bottom edges of the bag.

**5**

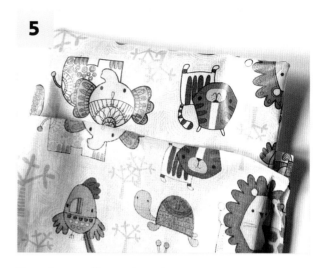

Turn the top flap right side out, and push the corners out to a point. You should have both bottom sides of the bag hanging with the wrong sides out.

**6**

The right side of the fabric is visible on the inside as well as the outside.

Turn one bag portion right side out, and slide the other bag inside it. Turn the raw edges inside, pin, and stitch together.

**7**

Top stitch the flap edge. Place the Velcro so it will line up when closed. Pin and stitch around the four sides of each piece of Velcro, and backstitch to reinforce.

# Intermediate Project 1: Drawstring Flat Pack

This funky twist on the plain drawstring bag can be made from a variety of fabrics—some good choices would be heavy cotton, corduroy, or lightweight denim. You can add varying design elements like I did, such as a lined zipper pocket, appliqué, and a contrasting band.

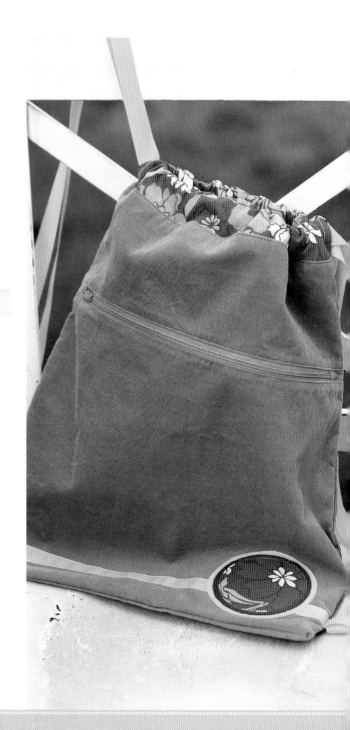

## What You Need

- Knowledge of straight seams, inserting a zipper, creating a casing, and sewing corners
- 18 x 45-inch (45.75 x 114.25 cm) piece cotton fabric for the main body
- 18 x 22-inch (45.75 x 56 cm) piece cotton fabric for the pocket lining
- Small piece cotton fabric for the contrast band
- Felt for the appliqué. (This design is made form two felt circles cut at 2.5-inch [6.25 cm] and 3-inch [7.5 cm] diameters.)
- 14-inch-long (35.5 cm) zipper
- 5 yards (457.25 cm) ⅝-inch-wide (1.5 cm) ribbon
- Straight and safety pins
- Measuring tape and ruler
- Iron
- Sewing machine

## Bag Pieces to Measure and Cut

- **Body back:** Cut 1 piece 15 x 17 inches (38 x 43 cm)

- **Top body front:** Cut 1 piece 4 ³⁄₄ x 15 inches (12 x 38 cm)

- **Lower body front:** Cut 1 piece 12 ¹⁄₄ x 15 inches (31 x 38 cm)

- **Zipper flaps:** Cut 2 pieces 1 x 1 ³⁄₄ inches (2.5 x 4.5 cm)

- **Drawstring casings:** Cut 2 pieces 4 x 15 inches (10 x 38 cm)

- **Pocket lining:** Cut 1 piece 15 x 17 inches (38 x 43 cm)

- **Ribbon:** Cut 2 pieces 72 inches (183 cm) long for straps; cut 2 pieces 3 ¹⁄₄ inches (7 cm) long for loops; cut 1 piece 15 inches (38 cm) long for bag front

*All seams are sewn at a ⁵⁄₈-inch (1.5 cm) seam allowance.

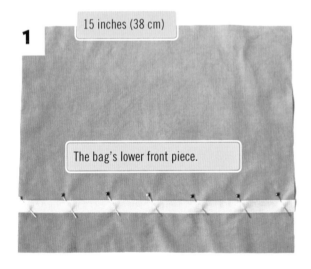

**1**

15 inches (38 cm)

The bag's lower front piece.

Place the bag's lower front right side up on your table. Position the piece of ribbon along the bottom of the fabric 3 inches (7.5 cm) up from the edge, and topstitch in place.

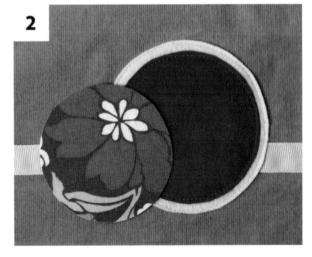

**2**

Cut out two felt circles and apply them to the front of the bag layered on top of each other.

**3**

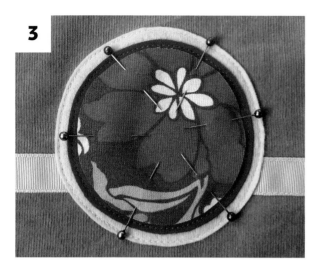

Cut at a 2-inch (5 cm) diameter circle from the cotton fabric. Pin it as the top layer of the appliqué, centered on top of the felt layers. Stitch around the edge of the circle.

**4**

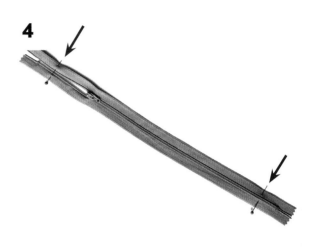

Measure 12 inches (30.5 cm) centered on the zipper. Mark the measurement with pins at each end.

**5**

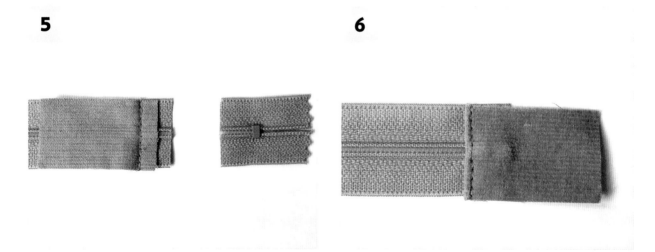

With the right side facing the top of the zipper, sew the zipper flap at the pin-marked spot. Trim off the end of the zipper.

**6**

Fold the fabric back, and topstitch to secure.

**7**

Repeat for the other end of the zipper. The zipper will need to be unzipped slightly so the fabric will fit under the sewing machine foot.

**8**

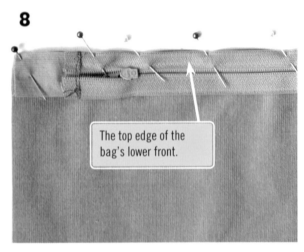

The top edge of the bag's lower front.

With the right sides together, place the zipper face down on the lower front piece. Line up the long side of the zipper with the top edge of the fabric. Pin and stitch with a zipper foot.

**9**

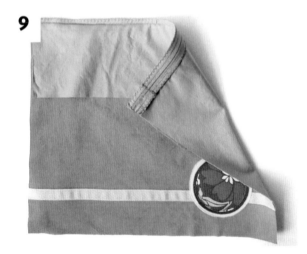

Turn the lower front so it is lying face up. Place the top front piece face down to line up with the other long side of the zipper. Pin and stitch in place. Zigzag stitch the edges to finish the seams.

**10**

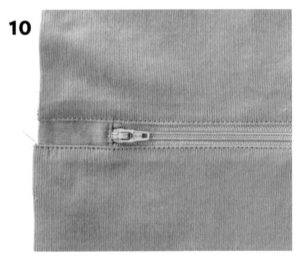

Fold the fabric open, and topstitch along both sides of the zipper. You still need to have the zipper foot attached to do this.

**11**

Place the entire front piece of the bag on top of the lining piece. The lining should be right side up, with the wrong side of the bag touching the lining. Baste stitch around the edges.

**12**

The loops should be facing in.

Take the two pieces of ribbon cut for the loops and fold them in half. Sew one at each end of the ribbon trim on the front of the bag.

**13**

The right sides are facing out.

Place the bag front on top of the bag back with the wrong sides together. Stitch with a ¼-inch (.6 cm) seam allowance around the sides and bottom edge of the bag, pivoting at the corners.

**14**

The raw edge of the seam is enclosed, creating a French seam for a clean finish!

Turn the bag inside out. Pin the edges of the bag on the sides and bottom. Straight stitch around the sides and bottom of the bag, this time at a ⅜-inch (.75 cm) seam allowance.

**15**

The yellow fabric shows the finished inside seam; the seam where blue meets blue is the outside of the bag.

Now that the main body of the bag is finished, set it aside to work on the drawstring casing.

**16**

Hem the short ends of the casing. Turn under ¼ inch (.6 cm), then ⅜ inch (.75 cm). Repeat for both ends of both pieces.

**17**

Fold the casing in half lengthwise with the right side out, and press.

**18**

Line up the raw edges of the casing strips with the top edge of the bag. The folded ends should meet at the side seams but not overlap. Pin and stitch.

**19**

Trim the seam, and finish the raw edge with a zigzag stitch to keep the fabric from fraying. Press the seam toward the bottom of the bag.

**20**

Topstitch along the top edge of the bag, being sure the seam points down so the casing lies flat.

**21**

Using a safety pin in the end of the ribbon, feed one of the straps through the front casing and into the back casing so both ends are loose on the same side.

**22**

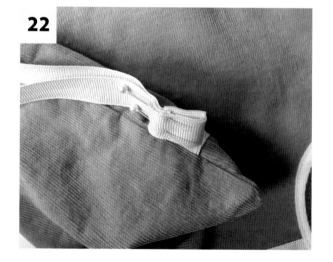

Feed the two ends through the same loop. Wrap around, fold the ends under, pin, and stitch to secure.

**23**

Repeat with the other ribbon strap, but feed the casing in through the other direction so the loose ends are on the opposite side. Now you can enjoy your finished bag!

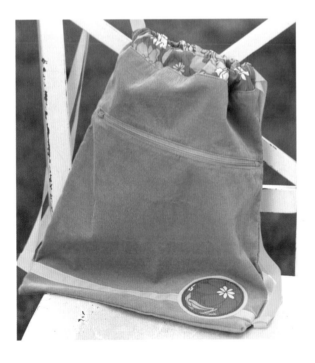

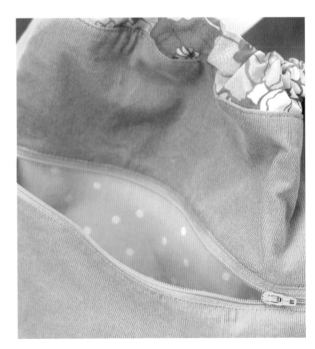

# Intermediate Project 2:
# Tablet Case

Use fabric and the skills you've learned to create a great-looking case for your tablet or eReader. This one is designed to look like a vintage envelope with an Old World-inspired feel and can easily be customized to fit any size tablet.

## What You Need

- Knowledge of straight seams, pivoting, sewing corners, appliqué, and attaching trim
- One 18 x 45-inch (45.75 x 114.25 cm) piece *or* two 18 x 22-inch (45.75 x 56 cm) pieces fabric
- Quilt batting *or* three felt sheets
- One 1 $^1/_2$-inch-wide (3.75 cm) and one $^1/_2$-inch-wide (1.25 cm) ribbon in different colors
- Two $^3/_4$-inch (2 cm) buttons
- 12-inch (30.5 cm) piece twine or string
- Measuring tape
- Scissors
- Pinking shears
- Stencil
- Air-soluble pen
- Straight pins
- Toothpick
- 8 x 3-inch (20×7.5 cm) piece fusible web, such as Heat and Bond

This example fits a 5×8-inch (12.75×20.25 cm) tablet.

### Tablet Pieces to Measure and Cut

- Trace your tablet on a piece of paper.

- Add $^3/_4$ inch (2 cm) to all sides of the rectangle for ease and a $^1/_2$-inch (1.25 cm) seam allowance. This creates the front pattern piece.

- Repeat tracing steps 1 and 2, measuring out 3 inches (7.5 cm) from the center of the line on the left side. Mark a point, and draw angled lines to each corner of the rectangle to create the flap extension. This creates the back pattern piece.

- Cut three layers for each piece—one of main fabric, one of lining fabric, and one or two of batting (depending on the thickness you want). If you're using felt instead of quilt batting, cut two layers and stack them together.

- Trim $^1/_2$ inch (1.25 cm) off the top edge (one long side) of the batting piece for the front.

**1**

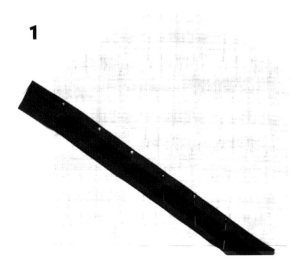

With the back piece right side up, stack the two pieces of ribbon and lay them diagonally across the rectangular area. Pin and stitch along the edges.

**2**

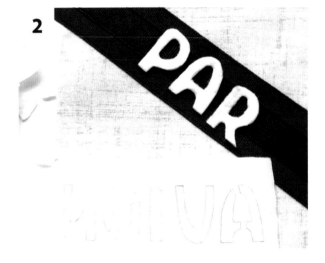

Apply fusible web to the backside of a piece of batting. Using a stencil, write the words "PAR AVION" backward on the paper backing. Cut out, and apply to the ribbon.

**3**

To create the stamp appliqué, cut a 2 × 2 ⅕-inch (5 × 6.25 cm) felt square with pinking shears, then cut a small piece of fabric for the top layer. Pin and topstitch around the edges.

**4**

Mark three wavy rows of stamp cancellation lines with an air-soluble pen, and stitch on top of those lines.

**5**

Place the top layer on top of the batting. Pin around the edges.

**6**

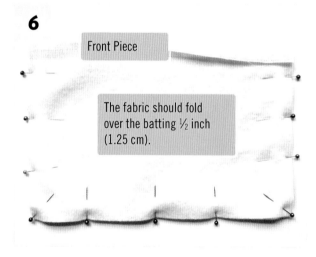

Front Piece

The fabric should fold over the batting ½ inch (1.25 cm).

Place the batting on the backside of the front piece. Trim the edge if necessary so the fabric extends ½ inch (1.25 cm) on one of the longer sides. Pin.

**7**

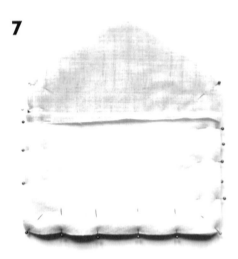

With the right sides together, lay the front piece on top of the back piece with the sides and bottom edge lined up. Straight stitch around the three edges.

**8**

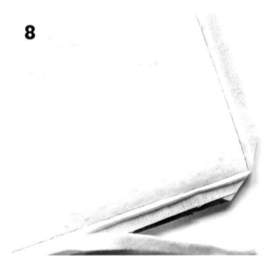

Grade the seam allowances by trimming the fabric and batting from the top front layers close to the seam. Clip the corners of the remaining fabric.

**9**

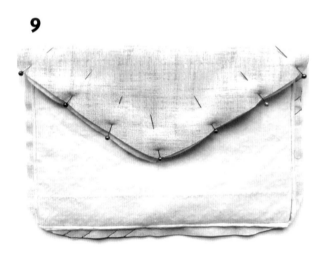

Fold the flap over, and pin the fabric to the batting. Notice the batting extends a bit; trim off the excess batting, and set aside.

**10**

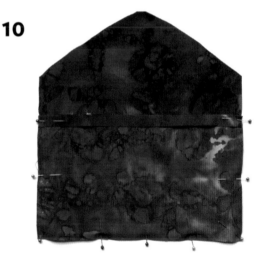

With the right sides together, sew the two lining pieces together. Fold the top edge of the front piece over ½ inch (1.25 cm), and stitch around the three sides.

**11**

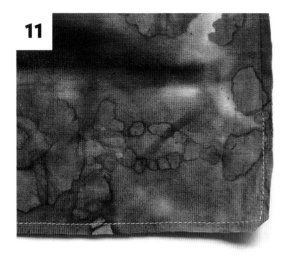

Trim the seam allowances and clip the corners of the lining fabric.

**12**

With the two flaps right sides together, place the lining on top of the main fabric. Pin around the edges of the flap, and stitch.

**13**

Trim the seam allowance, and turn the flap right side out. Push the corners to nice, crisp points. The pockets should still be inside out.

**14**

Turn the main fabric pocket right side out. Slide the lining pocket inside the main fabric.

**15**

Line up the top two edges that were previously folded under. Pin and topstitch the opening closed.

**16**

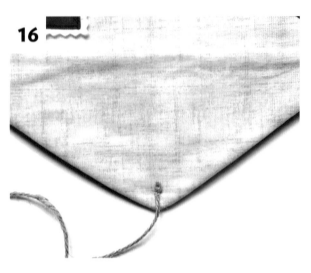

Sew the end of the twine ½ inch (1.25 cm) in from the edge of the flap point on the right side.

**17**

Use a toothpick to create a thread shank; this will provide space for the twine to wrap around.

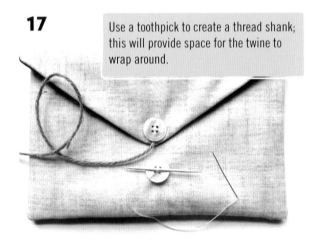

Sew one button over the end of the twine and another button on the front of the case, just below the point of the flap when it's folded over.

**18**

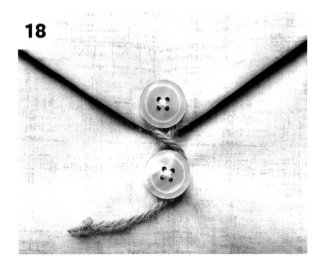

Wrap the twine around the two buttons in the motion of an eight to secure the flap closed. Open the case, and slide in your tablet.

# Intermediate Project 3:
# Picnic Blanket

Perfect for a picnic by the lake or a day down at the beach, this patchwork picnic blanket is a great project to test out your sewing skills. The 4 x 4 square design can be made from a variety of prints or colors. You can create a pattern or make it totally random.

Use quilting cotton for the top layer (fat quarters work great!) and a durable fabric like denim or a heavyweight twill for the bottom layer. The blanket has an attached built-in roll cover with a little handle to make it super easy to lug around.

## What You Need

- Knowledge of straight seams, buttonholes, and sewing corners
- Squares: 16 14 x 14-inch (35.5 x 35.5 cm) cotton fabric
- Backing: 54 $\frac{1}{2}$ x 54 $\frac{1}{2}$-inch (138.5 x 138.5 cm) denim fabric (it's best to buy a fabric that's 60 inches [152.5 cm] wide on the bolt)
- Roll cover: 2 rectangles 18×7-inch (45.75×17.75 cm) cotton fabric
- Handles: 2$\frac{1}{2}$×7-inch (6.25×17.75 cm) cotton fabric
- Ruler
- Measuring tape
- Scissors
- Iron
- Three buttons
- Ball of yarn

**1**

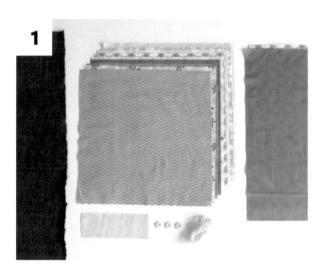

Measure and cut out all the pieces. All seams will be sewn at ½-inch (1.25 cm) seam allowance.

**2**

You can put the squares in any order.

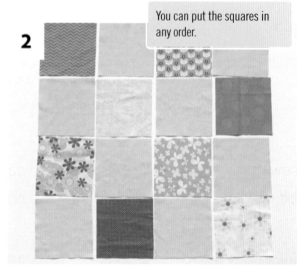

Lay out the 16 squares to determine your design.

**3**

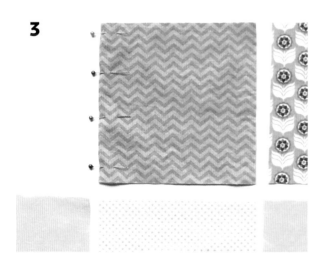

Start by sewing the top row of blocks together. Sew the center seam with the fabrics right side together and continue until you have four blocks connected into one row.

**4**

Press the seam allowances in the top row all in one direction. Press the next row's seam allowance in the opposite direction to make it easier to match the corners.

**5**

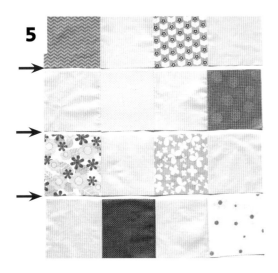

Repeat until you have four rows each with four blocks sewn together.

**6**

To connect the rows, with the right sides together, line up the raw edges of the first and second row, being sure to line up the seams for each block. Pin, and straight stitch.

**7**

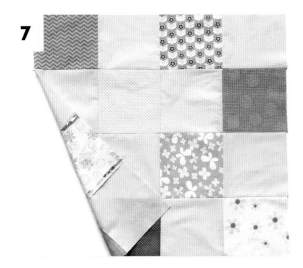

Repeat until all the rows are joined. Press the seams open.

**8**

Leave this space open for turning the blanket right side out.

With the right sides together, place the top layer on top of the backing fabric. Pin around the entire outside edge, leaving the sides of one block open to turn right side out.

**9**

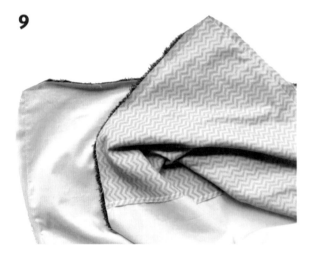

Sew around the pinned edge. Backstitch at the opening to reinforce the threads. Clip the seam allowances at the corners, and set aside.

**10**

To sew the handle, fold the handle fabric in half lengthwise, and sew a straight stitch down the long raw edge side. Turn it right side out, and press flat.

**11**

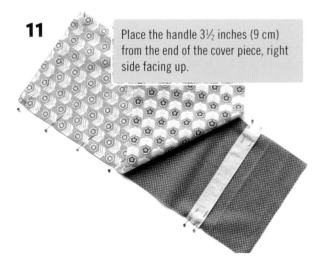

Place the handle 3½ inches (9 cm) from the end of the cover piece, right side facing up.

Topstitch the edges of the handle. Pin it in between the two cover pieces, right sides together. Pin and sew around three edges, leaving the end to the left open.

**12**

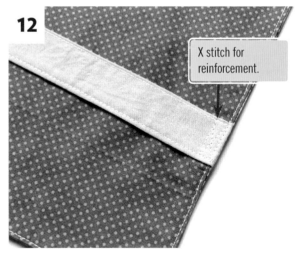

X stitch for reinforcement.

Sew an X to reinforce the ends of the handle. Topstitch around the edge of the cover piece.

**13**

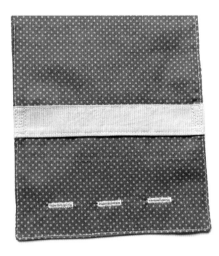

Sew three buttonholes 1 inch (2.5 cm) from the finished edge.

**14**

This is the left-open corner. Be sure to turn the edges inside to match the existing seam allowance.

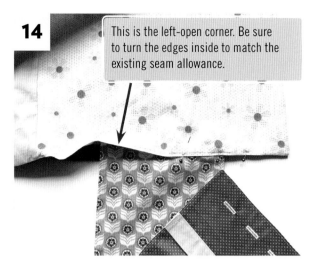

Place the open end of the cover in between the two layers of the blanket, centering it on the block. The side with the handle should be facing down, the same direction as the back layer. Pin and sew the opening closed.

**15**

Thread a large needle with yarn, and pull through both layers of the blanket at the points where the corners meet. Tie in knots to secure.

**16**

Fold the blanket in half, and fold it in half again so it is the width of one square. Roll up and wrap the cover around the blanket.

**17**

Mark the position of the three buttons to line up with the existing buttonholes. Sew the buttons in place, button up the cover, and you're ready to go!

# Intermediate Project 4: Makeup Brush Holder

Keep your makeup brushes clean and organized with this stylish roll-up fabric holder. The design accommodates six to eight brushes and keeps them secure in their own tiny pockets. The fabric folds over to protect them and rolls up for easy, grab-and-go style!

## What You Need

- Knowledge of straight seams, pivoting, sewing corners, and binding
- One 18×45-inch (45.75 × 114.25 cm) piece *or* three 18×22-inch (45.75 × 56 cm) pieces heavy fabric, such as denim. (Use three pieces if you want a contrasting exterior and interior.)
- 10×12-inch (25×30.5 cm) piece fusible nonwoven interfacing
- 48-inch-long (122 cm) extra-wide bias tape
- Scissors
- Sewing machine
- Measuring tape
- Straight pins
- Masking tape
- Iron
- Stiff, bristled brush (optional)

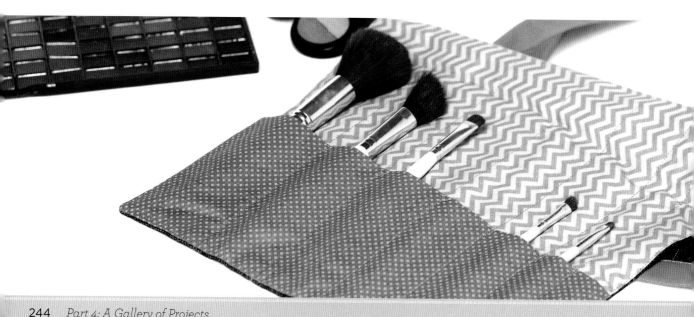

## Holder Pieces to Measure and Cut

- **Main body:** 2 pieces, each 13×19 inches (33×48.25 cm)
- **Pocket:** 1 piece, 13×11 inches (3×28 cm)
- **Interfacing:** 1 piece, 10×12 inches (25.5×30.5 cm)

**Note:** Since you're using a heavier fabric (I used denim) as the backing layer, you don't need to use interfacing here.

**1**

Apply the interfacing to the wrong side of the pocket. Center it so the seam allowances aren't covered.

**2**

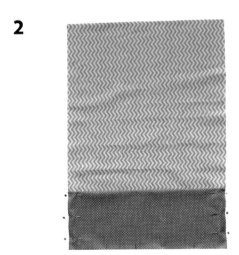

With the wrong sides together, fold the pocket in half, matching up the 13-inch-long (33 cm) sides. Pin the pocket to the bottom edge of the top layer of the body.

**3**

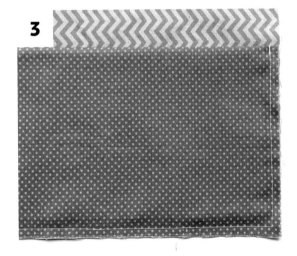

Using a ¼-inch (.6 cm) seam allowance, baste stitch the sides and bottom edge of the pocket. Pivot at the corners.

**4**

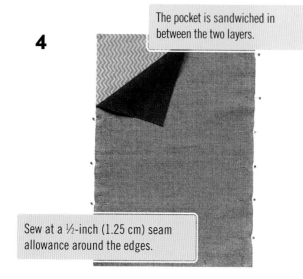

The pocket is sandwiched in between the two layers.

Sew at a ½-inch (1.25 cm) seam allowance around the edges.

Place the backing layer on top of the top layer, right sides together. Pin and stitch around the sides and bottom edge, leaving the top end open.

**5**

Trim the seam allowances at the bottom two corners. The larger stitching line that's visible is from previously basting the pocket; you should trim through that stitching line.

**6**

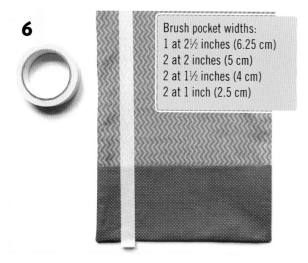

Brush pocket widths:
1 at 2½ inches (6.25 cm)
2 at 2 inches (5 cm)
2 at 1½ inches (4 cm)
2 at 1 inch (2.5 cm)

Use masking tape as a guide to sew a straight line. Measure 2 ½ inches (6.25 cm) from the left side to sew the first pocket line. The stitching line is sewn the entire length of the fabric.

**7**

Straight stitch along the edge of the tape. Stop when you get to the top edge of the pocket. Peel the tape up out of the way.

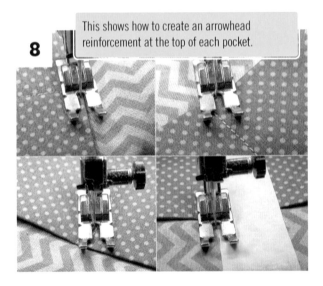

**8**

This shows how to create an arrowhead reinforcement at the top of each pocket.

Pivot the foot, and sew two stitches. Pivot, and sew diagonally back to the line. Pivot, and sew diagonally up to the top edge of the pocket. Pivot back to the center line.

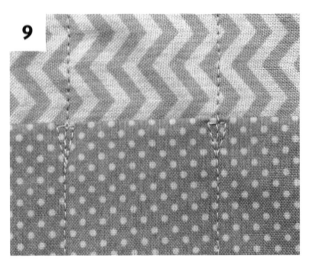

**9**

The pivoted shape should look like this when finished. The arrowhead reinforcement is optional, so feel free to skip if you like.

**10**

Continue to sew the rows of stitching to create the pockets, spacing the rows at the specified measurements. Each row of stitching should be sewn all the way at the open end.

**11**

Cut the bias tape to the length of the open end of the roll 12 ¼ inches (31 cm). Open it up, place it right sides down, pin, and sew along the fold line.

**12**

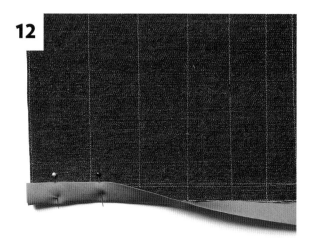

Turn the roll over, and fold the bias tape over to the backside. With the edge folded under, pin it so it's covering the raw edge of the fabric.

**13**

Topstitch along both long edges of the bias tape, leaving the short ends unsewn.

**14**

To make the tie, cut a 36-inch (91.5 cm) piece of the bias tape. Fold it in half, and topstitch the edges the entire length of the tie, leaving the short ends unsewn.

**15**

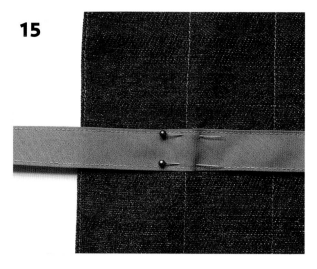

Measure 5 inches (12.75 cm) up from the end with the binding, and pin the center of the tie to the first stitching line. Stitch in place, lining the new stitching up with the existing stitching.

**16**

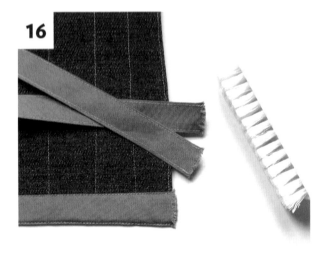

Take a stiff, bristled brush and brush over the ends of the bias tape to fray the ends. If you don't have a brush, pull at the threads to create a similar look.

**17**

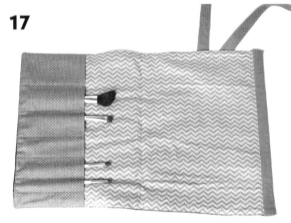

Slide the makeup brushes into the pockets.

**18**

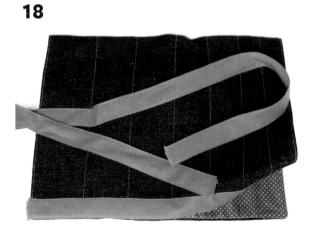

Fold the fabric over to cover the pocket with the brushes. Roll it up with the bias-trimmed end on the outside. Wrap the tie around it twice, and tie. You're all set!

# Intermediate Project 5:
# Appliqué Pillow

Creating a pillow is pretty simple. You sew two squares together, leaving a small space open for stuffing, and sew it closed with a few hand stitches to finish it up! You can make it in any size or shape—just make sure to cut both shapes the same size. You can embellish the pillow with an appliqué and add piping.

## What You Need

- Knowledge of straight seams, pivoting, sewing corners, appliqué, and attaching trim
- Two 18 x 18-inch (45.75 x 45.75 cm) pieces fabric (Quilting cotton is used here, but you can use any type of fabric that doesn't have stretch.)
- Scraps of fabric for appliqué
- One package or 90 inches (229 cm) piping
- 24-oz. package batting/polyfill
- 6 x 11-inch (15 x 28 cm) piece fusible web, such as Heat and Bond
- Measuring tape
- Scissors
- Sewing machine
- Fabric marking tool
- Zipper foot
- Hand-sewing needle
- Iron
- Seam ripper

**1**

Use a computer or hand draw the LOVE template. Trace these letters onto your fabric, and prepare the appliqué with fusible web. Cut out the letters and shapes.

**2**

To create the double appliqué heart, stack the first layer on a piece of felt. Bond with fusible web and trim around the edges to create a framed look.

**3**

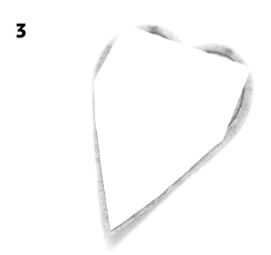

Cut out a small piece of the fusible web, and apply it to the back of the felt.

**4**

Mark the center of the pillow front with a pin or fabric marking tool. Position your letters until you are happy with the placement.

**5**

Peel off the paper backing, and bond the appliqué to the fabric with an iron. Allow it to cool completely before moving on to the next step.

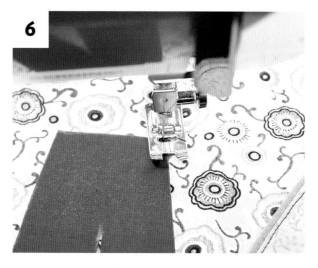

**6**

Stitch around the V using a satin stitch. The stitch should cover the raw edge of the appliqué fabric.

**7**

To select the satin stitch, set your machine to a zigzag and set the stitch length at zero. The stitching lines will be right next to each other.

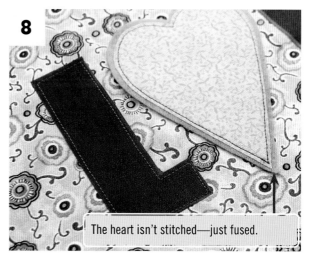

**8**

The heart isn't stitched—just fused.

Stitch using the raw edge appliqué technique for the L and E.

**9**

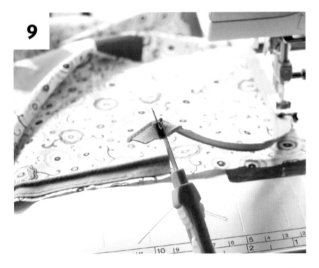

Apply the piping to the front side of the pillow. To join the ends, use a seam ripper to remove a few stitches at the end of the piping strip.

**10**

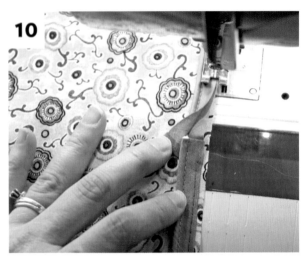

Open up the fabric to reveal the cord, and cut the cord back ½ inch (1.25 cm). Fold the raw end under, and overlap it with the other end of the piping.

**11**

Stitch along the edge to secure, and backstitch to reinforce.

**12**

With the right sides together, place the back of the pillow on top of the pillow front. Line up the edges, and stitch with a zipper foot.

**13**

Sew around the edge of the pillow, but leave a 4-inch (10 cm) opening on the side.

**14**

Trim the seams and clip the corner. Turn the pillow right side out.

**15**

Stuff the pillow by pushing in as much batting as you can through the opening.

**16**

Use a hand-sewing needle to sew the opening closed. Set your pillow out, and enjoy!

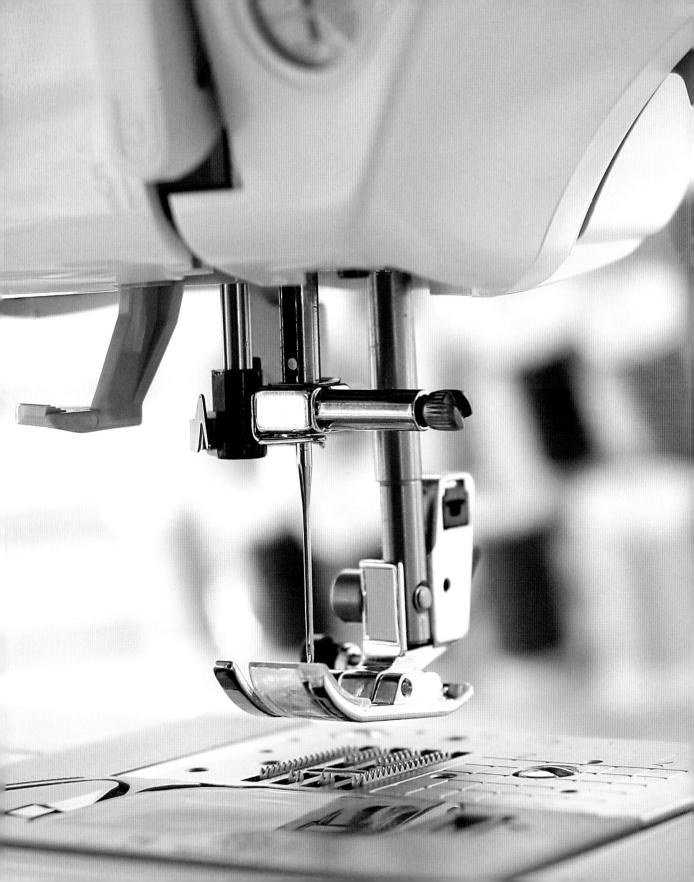

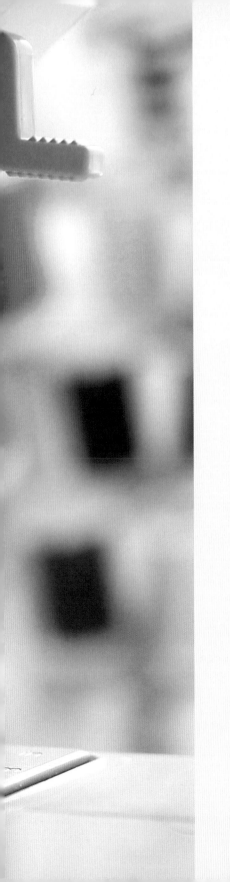

# Appendix

# Glossary

**appliqué**   Pieces cut from fabric, felt, or other materials that are then sewn onto a foundation fabric.

**backing**   The underside or lining in quilting.

**backstitch**   One or two firm stitches at the beginning or end of a row of stitching.

**ballpoint needle**   A sewing machine needle with a rounded tip that stitches knit fabrics without splitting the fabric.

**bar tacks**   A series of stitches used for reinforcing areas of stress, such as pocket openings or the bottom of a fly opening.

**baste**   A large running stitch done to temporarily hold pieces together during both fitting and construction.

**batting**   Insulating material between the top and bottom layers of the fabric commonly used in quilts or padded garments.

**bias**   The diagonal direction between the straight grain and the crossgrain. True bias is at a 45-degree angle.

**bias tape**   Tape made from strips of fabric cut on the bias. Bias tape is used for binding or facing seams.

**binding**   Finishing the raw edge of a garment by attaching a narrow strip of fabric that folds over to enclose the edge.

**bobbin**   A round spool holding the thread that forms the underside of a machine stitch.

**bolt**   A roll of fabric.

**boning**   Plastic strips slipped into sheaths that are sewn into a garment to give support and body contouring.

**casing**   A flat tube of fabric through which tape, elastic, or trim can be threaded.

**clip**   To cut into a seam allowance to mark a placement or allow a curve to spread and lie smooth.

**crosswise grain**   Fabric threads running from selvage to selvage.

**D-ring**   A D-shaped ring used as a fastener in belts and straps.

**dart**   A triangle-shaped tuck stitched into a garment that allows a fabric to shape to the contours of the body.

**drape**   The way fabric falls on the body.

**drawstring**   A cord or ribbon inserted through a hem or casing.

**dress form**   A torso-shaped frame used to fit garments during the construction process.

**ease**   An allowance added to a pattern for movement in a garment.

**edge stitching**   A row of stitching along the very edge of a garment or fold. Edge stitching is usually done about $\frac{1}{8}$ inch (.3 cm) or less from the edge.

**elastic thread**   Thin, polyester-wrapped thread used to make stretchable shirred fabric.

**embroidery hoop**   A pair of rings that keep fabric taut for embroidering.

**eyelet**   A small hole made in fabric. An eyelet is frequently finished with a buttonhole stitch or grommet.

**facing**   Fabric pieces either cut separately or folded back over themselves that enclose the raw edge of a garment.

**fastener**   Any method of closing a garment, such as a snap, zipper, or button.

**fat quarter**   A $\frac{1}{2}$ yard (45.75 cm) of fabric cut in half to make two quarters of a yard. Fat quarters usually measure 18×22 inches (45.75×56 cm), while a standard $\frac{1}{4}$-yard (23 cm) cut on a bolt is 9×44 inches (23×111.75 cm).

**feed dogs**   Metal teethlike ridges that emerge from rectangular holes in the throat plate of a sewing machine. Feed dogs gently grip the underneath of the fabric, helping it to move away as the stitches are sewn.

**fiberfill** Polyester fiber used for filling or insulation in pillows, comforters, and outerwear.

**finger press** Using your finger to mark and press a fold.

**finish** Turning under a raw edge and stitching it in place.

**fitting lines** Lines marked on a pattern that indicate the finished lines after sewing.

**flat-felled seam** Sewing the wrong sides of the fabric together and trimming one seam allowance close before turning the other seam under and stitching it over the first.

**fly wheel** The wheel that raises and lowers the sewing machine needle.

**fray** The loose threads on the edge of a fabric.

**free arm** A section on most sewing machines that can be removed from the base, allowing easier sewing of various types of projects—for example, when sewing around cuffs or hems of trousers.

**French seam** A seam stitched first with the wrong sides together, and then turned in and stitched with the right sides together so the raw edges are enclosed in the seam. This seam is often found in high-quality garments and is often used with sheer fabrics.

**frog closure** A fancy buttonlike closure for a garment. Frogs are usually ornamental and are made from silk ribbons or cords.

**fuse** To join two surfaces together with fusible tape.

**fusible tape** or **webbing** A heat-activated adhesive used to bond fabric.

**gather** To draw up a fabric by pulling rows of basting stitches in order to make it fit into a smaller, predetermined area.

**godet** An extra piece of fabric in the shape of a circular pie segment that's sewn into a seam to give added flare and volume. Godets are usually seen in dresses and skirts.

**grade** 1. Trimming one layer at a narrower width to reduce bulk in the seam allowance. 2. Altering a pattern to make it fit a smaller or larger size.

**grain** Indicates the direction of the yarn in fabric. The stronger lengthwise grain runs vertically parallel to the selvage, while the crosswise grain runs horizontally and has more give.

**grommet** A metal ring inserted into a hole in the fabric that helps reinforce openings used for lacings.

**grosgrain ribbon** A heavy corded ribbon characterized by its horizontal ribbed appearance.

**handwheel** The wheel that raises and lowers the sewing machine needle. *See also* fly wheel.

**hem** To finish the raw edge of a fabric by folding it over and stitching it down.

**hem line** On a pattern, the line that shows where the finished hem will be.

**Hong Kong binding** A binding that encloses the raw edges of the seams separately or individually inside strips of bias tape.

**interfacing** A textile used on the wrong side of the fabric to give support and help shape or stabilize where desired. Interfacing can be sewn in or fusible.

**interlining** A layer of fabric between the face and lining of a garment to give added warmth or body.

**jacquard** A fabric in which the design is intricately woven into the weave using a special loom.

**jeans needle** A strong needle for heavyweight fabrics, with a larger eye to accommodate thicker thread.

**knit** A fabric that consists of interlocking loops called stitches that can be made by hand or on a sewing machine.

**lining** A layer of fabric sewn to the inside of clothing that covers construction details and makes garments easier to put on and take off. Lining is usually made from a slick fabric.

**machine basting** A straight stitch sewn at the largest stitch length available. Machine basting is used to temporarily hold pieces together or create gathers.

**miter** The diagonal join of two edges at a corner used to finish the corners of garments or quilts.

**monofilament thread**   A clear, polyester or nylon thread used for hemming and quilting.

**muslin**   A cotton fabric made in various weights that's often used to make sewing patterns.

**nap**   Fabric that has a raised pile or texture to it, such as velvet or corduroy. Nap runs in one direction and requires all pattern pieces be cut in the same direction.

**needle plate**   Also called the *throat plate,* a metal or plastic plate on the base of the machine under the presser foot that has seam allowance markings to guide the fabric.

**nonwoven**   A fabriclike material made from long fibers bonded together by a chemical or heat process—for example, felt.

**notches**   Marking on a pattern used to line up two or more fabric pieces that will be joined together. Notches are symbolized in various sizes, from single to quadruple.

**notions**   A collective term for a variety of sewing accessories. Notions can refer to buttons, snaps, zippers, thread, pins, or seam rippers.

**one-way design**   Printed fabrics that have a directional pattern requiring special attention to be paid when cutting. All pieces must be facing in the same direction.

**overlock (serge)**   A quick method for finishing seams and edges in which you use a special machine called a *serger.* Edges are trimmed and covered with thread in one operation.

**patchwork**   Sewing strips or blocks of fabric together to make one larger piece. Patchwork is often used in quilting.

**pattern weights**   Small weights used in place of pins to hold the pattern to the fabric when cutting.

**pile**   The raised surface or nap of a fabric made by upright loops. Pile can be cut (as in velvet and corduroy) or left as loops (as in terry cloth).

**pinking shears**   Shears with notched blades used to finish the edges of fabric with a zigzag cut. Cuts made by these shears are done for decoration or to prevent raveling.

**piping cord**   A cord used inside a fold of fabric to create piping trim.

**pivot**   When sewing, to turn the corner by keeping the needle in the down position without cutting the thread.

**placket**   A finished opening found on shirt fronts, sleeve cuffs, skirt openings, dresses, and pants that's made to accommodate buttons, snaps, and other fasteners.

**press**   Using an iron in an up-and-down motion on one section of a fabric at a time without sliding the iron over it.

**presser foot**   The part of the sewing machine that rests on the fabric, pressing it down onto the feed dogs.

**pressing cloth**   A thin cotton fabric used in between the iron's surface and the fabric for protection.

**pressing ham**   A tightly stuffed, ham-shaped pillow used to press curved seams and darts.

**raglan**   A type of sleeve with a seam that runs diagonally down from the neckline to the underarm. A raglan is made separately and then attached to a garment.

**raw edge**   The unfinished, undecorated edge of a fabric.

**ribbing**   A fabric trim knitted to create ribs for stretchability. Ribbing is commonly used for cuffs and waistbands.

**right side**   The finished side of a fabric.

**rise**   The distance between the crotch and waistband in pants, shorts, and underwear.

**rotary cutter**   A tool with a sharp, circular blade used to cut fabric.

**rotary cutting ruler**   A metal or hard plastic ruler used to guide a rotary cutter.

**ruffle**   A strip of fabric that's cut and gathered in such a way as to create fullness.

**running stitch**   A basic stitch in hand sewing and embroidery that's created by passing a needle in and out of a fabric.

**seam**   The point at which two layers of fabric are sewn together.

**seam allowance**   The amount of fabric between the seam and the cut edge.

**selvage**   The tightly woven edge of a fabric along the lengthwise grain.

**serge**   To finish the edges of a fabric with a serger.

**set-in sleeve**   A sleeve made separately and then joined to the body of a garment by a seam that starts at the under-arm and continues all the way around the armhole.

**shank (button)**   Created by using a premade attached shank button or thread shank. The shank raises the button above the garment, allowing the buttonhole space under the button to lie flat in order to avoid distortion of the garment.

**shirring**   Parallel rows of gathered stitches. Shirring can also be done with elastic thread.

**shrinkage**   When a fabric or garment becomes smaller than its original size, usually through laundering.

**slipstitch**   A hand stitch sewn from right to left used to join two folded edges together with very small, hardly vis-ible stitches.

**smocking**   An embroidery technique using decorative stitching to hold rows of small pleats. Smocking is usually sewn in a bodice.

**stabilizer**   Materials used in sewing to hold fabric flat so it's more easily stitched. Interfacing can act as a stabilizer.

**staystitching**   A row of stitches around a curve used to keep the curve from becoming distorted while sewing.

**stitch in the ditch**   Stitching right into the seam where the two fabrics meet, so the stitching is barely visible.

**tack**   Similar to baste, large stitches used to temporarily hold the fabric in place and then removed after the final stitching is complete.

**tailor's chalk**   A small piece of hard chalk used to mark on fabric.

**tailor's ham**   *See* pressing ham.

**tension**   The pressure placed on both the upper and lower threads while machine sewing.

**topstitch**   Finished stitching on the right side of a fabric.

**tuck**   A narrow pleat sewn down the length of the fold, often done in rows.

**turn out**   Turning a project or piece of clothing to the right side.

**twill tape**   A packaged cotton fabric tape made from a diagonal weave.

**underlining**   A layer of fabric placed behind each fabric piece to stabilize and hide construction details.

**understitch**   A stitch used to sew the facing to the seam allowance, but not the finished layer of the garment. Understitching keeps the facing from rolling out to the right side.

**Velcro**   The brand name for a common hook-and-loop fastener.

**vent**   The opening on the lower part of the back of a jacket or skirt that has a facing.

**walking foot**   A sewing machine foot used to guide sev-eral layers of fabric under the foot together as one unit. It prevents the fabrics from being pulled apart or shifting.

**warp**   The lengthwise grain of a fabric.

**weft**   The crosswise grain of a fabric.

**welt**   A narrow strip of fabric used to reinforce an edge or opening. It's often found in a welt pocket.

**woven**   A type of fabric made by weaving yarn on a loom.

**wrong side**   The inside or backside of a piece of fabric; the unfinished side.

**yoke**   Usually found at the neck or waist of a garment, the fitted piece that attaches to the hanging portion of the garment.

**zigzag**   A machine stitch sewn from side to side.

**zipper foot**   A sewing machine presser foot used to sew a zipper or other trims with raised edges.

# Index

## A

appliqué, 140-143
    basic appliqué steps, 141-142
    double layer, 140, 142
    fusible web, 141
    printed fabric, 142
    raw edge, 140
    reverse appliqué steps, 143
    satin stitch, 140
    styles, 140
    template, 141

## B

backstitch, 37, 42
    button, 37
    purpose, 37
    steps, 37
basting
    collar, 164
    curved hems, 172
    gathering a ruffle, 90
    purpose, 37
beaded trim, 70
bias, 10
bias tape, 76-79
    binding edges, 76-77
    blanket binding, 82
    double fold, 82
    extra-wide double-fold bias, 76
    making your own, 80-83
    materials needed, 76
    mitering a corner, 79
    purposes, 76
    quilt binding, 82
    sewing a bias tape hem, 78
    single fold, 82
    stitch in the ditch, 77
    types of, 82

blanket binding, 82
blanket stitch, 43
blind hem stitch, 43
blind stitch foot, 29
bobbin housing, 18
bobbin loading, 24-27
    bobbin types, 25
    bobbin winder, 25
    diagram, 24
    front-loading bobbin, 27
    machine manual, 24
    needle plate, 27
    steps, 25
    top-loading bobbin, 26
bobbin thread guide, 18
bobbin winder, 18
box pleats, 128-129
    marking, 128
    materials needed, 128
    pressing, 129
    purposes, 128
    steps, 128-129
braided trims, 70
button fitting foot, 28
buttonhole foot, 29, 110-113
    automatic buttonhole, 110
    diagram, 110
    machine stitching, 112
    marking, 112
    materials needed, 110
    presser foot, 113
    steps, 111-113
    stitch setting, 111
buttonhole lever, 19
buttonhole opening, 114-115
    button types, 115
    button uses, 114
    embroidery scissors, 114
    materials needed, 114
    steps, 114-115

button sewing, 116-117
    four-hole button, 116
    hand sewing, 116
    handwheel, 117
    machine sewing, 117
    shank button, 116
    two-hole button, 116

## C

catch stitch, 42
channel and diamond quilting, 148
clothing techniques, 156-177
    collar attachment, 163-165
    curved hems, 172-173
    French seams, 174-175
    interfacing, 158-159
    pockets, 160-162
    setting a sleeve, 166-167
    waistband, 168-171
cloth-marking pencils, 7
collar attachment, 163-165
    basting, 164
    facing pieces, 164
    grading, 165
    materials needed, 163
    pinning, 164
    simplest type of collar, 163
    snipping, 163
    steps, 163-165
cording foot, 29
corduroy, 13
corners and curves, 56-67
    corners, 62-65
    curved seams, 58-61
crocheted lace, 70
curved hems, 172-173
    basting, 172
    marking, 172
    materials needed, 172

French seams, 174-175
    description, 174
    fabric direction, 174
    fabric type, 174
    inside view, 175
    loose threads, 175
    materials needed, 174
    pressing, 174
    steps, 174-175
front-loading bobbin, 27
fusible interfacing, 145, 158-159
fusible web, 136, 141

## G–H

gathers. *See* ruffles and gathers
grain line, 183
grosgrain, 70

hand-sewing needles, 6
handwheel, 18, 19
hems, curved, 172-173. *See also* seams
  and hems
    basting, 172
    marking, 172
    materials needed, 172
    pressing, 173
    steps, 172-173
high-quality thread, 22
hook closure, 171
hooks and eyes, 118
    common place to use, 118
    description, 118
    hook and bar closure, 118
    steps, 118

## I–J

interfacing, 158-159
    colors, 158-159
    fusible, 145, 158-159
    glue, 168
    knit interfacing, 159
    nonwoven interfacing, 159

    purposes, 158
    selection, 159
    sew-in, 158-159
    types, 158
    weights, 158
    woven interfacing, 159
invisible zipper foot, 29
ironing board, 9

jersey needles, 23

## K–L

knife pleats, 126-127
    folding of fabric, 126
    materials needed, 126
    pinning, 126
    pressing, 127
    ruler, 126
    steps, 126-127
knits, 12-13
    interfacing, 159
    knit stretch, 12
    warp knit, 12
    weft knit, 12
    wovens versus knits, 12

lace, 70
large prints, yardage adjustment for, 11

## M

magnetic pincushion, 6
measuring tools, 7
    clear, plastic ruler, 7
    cloth-marking pencils, 7
    flexible tape measure, 7
    seam gauge, 7
    water-erasable marker, 7
metallic lace, 70
monogramming foot, 29

## N–O

needle
    eye, 40
    faulty, 39
    hand-sewing, 6
    machine sewing, 23
    position, 18, 61
    threader, 6,18, 40
    threading, 40
nonwoven interfacing, 159
notches, 169, 182
notions, preshrinking of, 14

operation panel, 18
outline quilting, 150
overcasting foot, 28

## P

paper scissors, 8
patterns, 178-185
    laying out and cutting, 184-185
    markings, 182-183
    multi-size, 132
    reading the envelope, 180-181
pinking shears, 8, 50
pins and needles, 6
    hand-sewing needles, 6
    magnetic pincushion, 6
    needle threader, 6
    safety pins, 6
    straight pins, 6
    stuffed pincushion, 6
piping, 70, 74-75
    bias strips, 74
    common use, 74
    definition, 74
    materials needed, 74
    premade, 74
    steps, 74-75
pivoting, 63
plaids, yardage adjustment for, 11
pleated grosgrain ribbon, 70